X-FORMATION

X FORMATION

Transforming Business Through Interim Executive Leadership

A Definitive Guide

DAMON NETH WILLIAM MINCE JIM TRELEAVEN

FOREWORD AND CONTRIBUTIONS BY ROBERT JORDAN AND OLIVIA WOLAK

X-FORMATION
Transforming Business Through Interim Executive Leadership

ISBN 978-1-5445-0045-4 *Hardcover*
978-1-5445-0046-1 *Ebook*

Cover art concept created by Park Jarrett IV.

Dedicated to our families for their love and support, and our clients who provided a wealth of life experiences that made this book possible.

—DAMON, WILLIAM, AND JIM

CONTENTS

FOREWORD

We've all heard people say, "Those were the days," looking back on previous generations and idealizing a simpler life. In our parents' generation, managers worked at the same company their entire careers, opting for stability and a guaranteed paycheck. It was the safe route. But time has passed, and our world is faster and more fluid, pliable, volatile, and complex. Into this new world, the interim specialty has emerged as companies seek leadership solutions that will drive progress and forward movement in the face of confusion and uncertainty.

Interim Executives are a unique set of leaders who bring clarity, confidence and results to many organizations worldwide. They love a good challenge and choose a career path that is anything but stable, going from assignment to assignment to grow and sometimes turn around organizations in need.

In an effort to seek out the best-in-class Interim Executives in the world, we formed what would eventually become InterimExecs and the Association of Interim Executives in 2009. Since then, we have screened over five thousand executives around the world to form an elite team of Interims who are deployed into companies in need of leadership resources. We call this the RED Team, RED standing for Rapid Executive Deployment. Authors of this book, Damon Neth, Jim Treleaven, and Bill Mince are among the executives who made the cut, each having great track records taking on interim assignments in their unique areas of expertise.

Damon, Bill, and Jim got to know each other thanks to their participation on the RED Team. They understand what it takes to successfully operate as Interim Executives, bringing measurable results to organizations. As we've gotten to know each other, our conversations tended to come back to a central point about the lack of awareness and understanding of this emerging leadership specialty among the general business public.

These conversations led Damon, Bill, and Jim to do something about it.

They decided to solve the problem by putting their combined years of experience together to publish the book you now hold. Just the fact of its publication is proof of the power of expert operating executives: they take action. They quickly assess a situation, figure out a plan of action, and then move forward.

More than one year of effort and thinking went into the writing of this book, combining over one hundred years of management wisdom. One of very few resources ever published anywhere in the world on the subject of interim leadership, Bill, Damon and Jim have done the business community a service by covering all aspects of the interim leadership model, both from the point of view of the organization utilizing this on-demand executive talent model and the executive seeking to learn more.

Whether you read this book in whole or in part, you'll benefit. Interim executive leadership may be one manifestation of the evolving workplace, but as more businesses opt to make operational upgrades and innovate, streamline technology, and position themselves in new and uncharted markets, on-demand and project based talent needs will arise to help through these points of transformation. There is much to learn from Interim Executives both in how they parachute into organizations, immediately taking action, and in how they structure project-based assignments for maximum impact.

Thank you to Damon, Bill, and Jim for providing a work of art that will expand the reader's worldview of business and empower organizations around the globe to demand the best of their leaders.

INTRODUCTION

As the Red Queen told Alice, "My dear, here we must run as fast as we can, just to stay in place. And if you wish to go anywhere you must run twice as fast as that."[1] This is true for many companies—they must keep pace, or the competition will leave them behind. Change creates opportunity and risk, requiring strength in strategy, planning, and execution across the organization. Starting at the top.

Ninety-six percent of all companies fail before their tenth birthday.[2] Companies with once great products, processes, people, and technology have been caught flat-footed, losing out to more nimble competitors. Even after ten years of survival, some of the most dominant companies can and do fail, as demonstrated by the headline-grabbing failure of

1 Lewis Carroll, *Alice's Adventures in Wonderland & Other Stories* (New York: Barnes & Noble Books), 2010.

2 Bill Carmody, "Why 96% of Businesses Fail within 10 Years" Inc.com, August 12, 2015.

stalwarts like Circuit City, Netscape, Woolworths, Sharper Image retail stores, Kodak, and many other once strong industry leaders. The need for constant innovation can challenge solid and well-established executive teams as needs change and the company enters unchartered territories.

In addition to the traditional challenges of business, sometimes life throws curveballs, creating the need for an immediate change in the executive ranks. These situations are particularly difficult for organizations that are struggling, often resulting in compromised decision-making or loss of focus on the primary must haves for success in a given executive role. Sometimes that company may not entirely understand how to define excellence, the role or accountability for the function. Sometimes companies suffer from enterprise-wide dysfunction due to poor understanding of vision, lack of clarity related to how to best organize departments and define each role's unique value to core processes, or complacency with so-so results. If that was not enough, the need for constant innovation demands continuous fresh thinking at the top.

These factors can impact an organization's ability to find a great executive in a timely manner. It creates hardship in the form of long searches that stretch on or short searches that result in a hasty hire. Sudden or unexpected executive needs can create the risk that the organization will slow or halt progress on important initiatives while other key resources cover for the missing executive. Moreover, there is the risk that the ultimate selection simply will not work out, consuming more resources and losing additional time as the organization returns to square one.

Welcome the Interim Executive. X-FormationTM, the art and science of critical or large-scale Transformation, captures the nature of who an Interim is, what an Interim does and why an Interim makes sense in today's fast-moving business environment. Interim Executives ("Interims" for short) are transformational tools used by a company to make powerful changes to its business. Interims are change agents who confidently lead organizations to higher ground, introduce new ways of thinking and doing business, and create repeatable success. Interims embody the x factor their clients need.

Interim Executive is a new form of career that originated in the Netherlands, spreading across Europe to the US and other areas of the world. Interims are seasoned best-in-class executives, helping companies to solve complex challenges, to move into unfamiliar territories, and to achieve stronger results. They assume an active leadership role for their clients by working as a contractor either fractionally or full time for a nonpermanent duration. Interim help is often available on short notice, with many new assignments starting within days of finding the right candidate.

Quality Interims have deep domain expertise, allowing them

to help companies solve long-term and complex problems by diving in without hesitancy (entering the danger), by tackling challenges head-on, and by implementing best practice solutions to companies in need. Thus, they are able to lead organizations to new heights through transformation. They also serve as mentors to other executives and key people in the organization, teaching new tools and approaches, and leading by example.

The typical characteristics of an Interim Executive will include many of the following:

- Decades of executive experience reporting to the CEO, board of directors, and Founder
- Executive experience at diverse organizations, often with Fortune 500, or other very large/complex companies
- Ground-up development and execution of strategic initiatives and plans
- Fundraising for startups and participation in an IPO
- Multiple Merger and Acquisition (M&A) transactions focused on market analysis, due diligence, negotiation, and post-acquisition integration
- Innovation expertise as evidenced by awarded patents or intellectual property (IP)
- Product, product line, and sales channel definition, expansion, and innovation
- Startup of new divisions or business sectors and expansion into new geographies

- Entrepreneurial experience as founder or equity owner in companies typically having orchestrated successful exits
- Published author, lecturer, or national speaker
- Postgraduate degree in a business concentration such as finance, economics, or technology
- Excellent self-awareness with the ability to bring out the best in others
- A passion for driving results and making tough decisions
- Deep domain experience in the industry or required functional area
- A diverse set of skills with the ability to be an agent of change when needed
- An extensive list of experiences and clients, with references available when required
- And, most importantly, a proven track record of success in industry and as an Interim Executive

There is no single skillset that defines an Interim, but an Interim is typically not someone who has simply held a senior-level title working in industry or consulting. The best Interims have held operational roles in the C-suite (CEO, CFO, CIO, COO, CMO, etc.) before taking on interim assignments or fractional engagements that benefitted from their unique skills and worldview. Not to be confused with board members who sometimes temporarily step in as placeholders taking an interim title, career Interims are true change agents. Their real strength is their experience and willingness to jump into the pilot's seat and lead the organization in whatever course corrections and improvements that are needed, bringing with them great energy, fresh perspectives, sound decision-making, and a proven track record of success.

Why do such talented individuals pursue careers as Interims rather than traditional permanent executive positions? First, as mentioned earlier, virtually all Interims have had successful careers in traditional permanent positions. For a number of reasons, including variety of work, flexibility, and continual challenge, some individuals choose interim work as a career. It's important to note that career Interims do not view their work as a temporary activity undertaken while awaiting the next permanent position. Rather, it's a very conscious career choice. While atypical, all true Interims share a characteristic of desiring, and essentially needing, constant change and challenges in their diet, which is one reason they tend to not take permanent positions with their clients, despite frequently being asked to assume ongoing roles.

Interims represent the ultimate end state of the personal, or "gig," economy, allowing these high performers to contribute specialized value to companies in line with their best and highest use. An organization, in turn, benefits by matching its specific high-level needs with a tailor-made executive who brings far fewer complexities and risks than a traditional permanent executive. An assertion supported by the Intuit 2020 Report:

> Traditional employment will no longer be the norm, replaced by contingent workers such as freelancers and part-time workers. The long-term trend of hiring contingent workers will continue to accelerate with more than 80 percent of large companies planning to substantially increase their use of a flexible workforce.[3]

In addition to filling the immediate need to take executive control due to a vacancy in the organization, Interims add value in many types of circumstances, bringing deep domain expertise to difficult business challenges or opportunities.

Some examples include:

- Expanding into unfamiliar territory (geographies, markets, products, etc.)
- Successfully scaling with rapid growth or expansion
- Retaining high performance / quality during hyper growth
- Breaking out of parochial or internally focused management and decision-making
- Addressing stalled growth
- Filling gaps in the management team (bandwidth, skills, or ability to solve major issues)

---

3 "Intuit 2020 Report: Twenty Trends That Will Shape the Next Decade," *Intuit.com*, October 2010, http-download.intuit.com/http.intuit/CMO/intuit/futureofsmallbusiness/intuit_2020_report.pdf.

- Planning and executing a turnaround, often when the survival of the company is at stake
- Developing succession plans
- Correcting poor financial performance
- Innovating and optimizing processes to fix quality issues, scale limitations, or poor gross margins
- Developing realistic strategy
- Reinventing the customer satisfaction/experience (especially if poor)
- Integrating acquisition(s) and new operations or lines of business
- Driving innovation and fresh thinking in products or services

Interim Executives walk into situations where the results matter and the consequences are high. They employ world-class strategic and tactical skills to lead a company to where it needs to be in the shortest amount of time possible. Once the *X-Formation* is complete, Interims smoothly exit an organization, in many cases helping define the go-forward role and hiring their replacement. They bolster the value to the client at the end of an engagement by proactively addressing transition plans and pacing their efforts with remaining needs, always ensuring that they continue to address important work and to deliver needed value winding down an engagement.

> Interim Executives understand that time is money and hit the ground running, with an action-oriented approach focused on creating tangible results with no energy to waste on political battles, arguments, and inefficiency.

This book outlines all facets of Interim Executive leadership, helping readers learn what Interims are and the skillsets they possess, how they approach the job and create value for their clients, and how Interims are found and engaged. For simplicity, we will refer to these C-level executives throughout the rest of the book as "Interims." The book has been arranged into sections so you can skip ahead to a section or chapter based on topics of interest or level of understanding of the Interim Executive model.

Section 1 explains Interim leadership and how it is different from traditional consulting services. Interims are leaders and decision-makers who focus on execution and take an organization-wide purview when assessing opportunities for innovation and change. They revitalize your staff and make the hard decisions that are needed to create rapid improvement. They are typically board members or possess similar senior leadership experience, providing them with the ability to assist with strategic and tactical issues from day one. Experienced Interims use a big tool box full of proven approaches, best practices, and leadership know-how to meaningfully help companies address stubborn challenges. They understand that time is money and hit the ground running, with an action-oriented approach focused on creating tangible results with no energy to waste on political battles, arguments, and inefficiency.

Section 2 provides details of how Interims develop strategies and tactics to bring about needed improvements for their clients. Above all else, Interims focus on execution and delivering tangible results, targeting the four *X-Formation* execution disciplines: strategize, optimize, maximize, and organize. Interims turn strategy into plans and plans into action. They utilize the depth and breadth of their experiences to drive deep transformation, unleashing the hidden value in existing products, processes, and systems. They focus on achieving complete results, looking at value and supply chains holistically through the lens of strategic planning, change management, execution/efficiency, cost reduction, revenue growth, market positioning, organizational structure, and culture.

Section 3 details the principles involved in finding an Interim, assessing his or her fit to your needs, creating an agreement and preparing for a successful start to the engagement. Interims are not run-of-the-mill consultants. They have unique world views, crave change and transformation, and often have nontraditional résumés. This section details how to assess the fit of an Interim based on a large number of complex considerations. Section 3 further outlines the elements of an engagement, including defining the role, effort, accountability, schedule, and cost. It shows how to prepare for an Interim with examples for defining your needs, goals, time frame, and budget, and finally negotiating a contract. Although the involvement of an Interim makes sense for most companies in many different scenarios, Chapter 11 outlines cases where Interim leadership may not be the best approach.

Throughout this book, you will find case studies illustrating real-world examples of companies, their needs, and Interim assignments. Many of these case studies and the results delivered are from the firsthand experiences of the authors of this book and the clients they have served. Collectively, hundreds of clients have benefitted from the authors' Interim Executive intervention. The content within conveys real-world experiences and not theory about how Interims positively transform organizations.

This book also presents groundbreaking research on the factors that matter most in assessing the fit of an Interim to your organization and its needs. These findings, and the resulting framework presented in Chapter 10, "Assess," are the result of years of real-world interactions with Interims and the companies that utilize them as presented by InterimExecs, the premier membership organization for Interims in the United States, and its exclusive Rapid Executive Deployment (RED) Team. While all the authors are members of InterimExecs and the RED Team, the ideas presented here are their independent ideas regarding interim excellence based on their experience.

After reading this book, you will have a full understanding of the profile of an Interim, how to know when one can help, the details of what they do, and the process of locating and engaging a great Interim.

SECTION 1

WHAT IS INTERIM LEADERSHIP?

Interim Executives are best described as high-performance Swiss Army knives for business. They operate in many ways as very senior consultants, but with the leadership and accountability that traditionally has only been present in permanent executive-level roles. They quickly identify key issues and lead organizations through the changes necessary to accomplish important goals, oftentimes in situations where everything is on the line. They possess a large array of real-world experiences and a track record of successes, often spanning many industries.

The business case for the use of Interim Executives is well established in Europe, where companies have been using this class of specialized problem solver for decades to great effect. According to Randstad's recent forecast of the 2025 European workplace, the number of companies creating this type of agile workforce model has increased from 18 percent in 2012 to 46 percent in 2016.[4] This trend is being driven by talent shortages and globalization, with Randstad further drawing the conclusion that, "as early as 2019, as much as 50 percent of the [US] workforce will be comprised of agile workers, as nearly 4 in 10 (39 percent) workers say they are likely to consider shifting to an agile arrangement over the next two-to-three years."[5] The Interim model and supporting value proposition has now spread to North America, where organizations with revenues ranging from less than $1 million to $1 billion-plus are now utilizing Interims and reaping the benefits.

In this section you will learn from the firsthand experiences of Interims and their clients, detailing the large and meaningful challenges or opportunities that these organizations faced and the transformational results an Interim helped deliver. Section 1 further defines qualities of experienced Interims, the difference between Interims and consultants, and the business case that is driving the expanded use of Interim Executives due to the value they create.

4 "Randstad Workplace 2025 Executive Summary," Randstadusa.com, 2016.

5 "Randstad US Study Projects Massive Shift to Agile Employment and Staffing Model in the Next Decade," Randstadusa.com, December 12, 2016, https://www.randstadusa.com/about/news/randstad-us-study-projects-massive-shift-to-agile-employment-and-staffing-model-in-the-next-decade/.

CHAPTER 1

MINI CASES

SEVEN SIGNS AN INTERIM CAN HELP

An Interim Executive is an important tool that an organization can use to effectively address a variety of pressing needs, capitalize on new opportunities, address stubborn problems, and provide solid leadership through catastrophic situations. Interims focus on solving problems and transforming companies, helping each client accomplish previously unattainable results.

The most common understanding of the role of an Interim is to fill an immediate need in the executive team caused by a sudden voluntary or involuntary departure by a permanent leader. In this case, a seasoned executive can step right in and enable the company to progress unabated; however, there are many other instances in which Interim Executive leadership makes sense.

Interims are leaders who have a heavy focus on execution and getting the job done. In Section 2 we detail the four Key *X-Formation* disciplines of strategize, optimize, maximize, and organize, showing how experienced Interims get results. Most assignments require an Interim to focus on many or all of these execution disciplines. The following case studies outline real-world examples in which companies utilized the help of an Interim Executive to achieve game-changing results and employed the *X-Formation* disciplines to lead the company through the changes needed.

GROWING TOO FAST: OUTGROWING THE EXECUTIVE TEAM

A successful professional services business was growing rapidly as a result of both organic growth and a series of small acquisitions but was struggling to realize the value of this strategy. Most of the C-level executives, including the CEO, CMO, and COO, were very experienced and capable of running a much larger company, but the missing piece was an experienced CFO. Like many small companies, a traditional controller had been more than adequate at smaller scale, but the company's new growth and acquisition strategy exceeded the experience and skills of the controller.

The CEO, seeing the broader opportunity, chose to bring in an Interim CFO to manage the acquisition of a number of smaller companies, to evaluate the requirements for a permanent CFO, and ultimately to recruit the long-term CFO. The Interim had served on a board with the CEO in the past, which helped the process move quickly. The Interim was onboard helping the team within two weeks.

The Interim CFO quickly assessed where previous acquisitions failed to deliver the anticipated value. He was then able to build plans that allowed the company to manage all aspects of several small acquisitions, including due diligence, legal, financial, and integration. The Interim, drawing on his experience in scaling through acquisition, was able to put in place the processes and systems to facilitate subsequent acquisitions.

Together with the CEO, the Interim developed a job description for a permanent CFO appropriate to the expected future requirements of the business. The Interim successfully recruited and hired a permanent CFO with a long track record of delivering solid results for similar organizations, locking in the value that the Interim had created and facilitating a smooth exit.

WHO'S NEXT? SUCCESSION PLANNING

A large marketing services firm was founded by a very successful CEO with extensive experience in the industry. A serial entrepreneur, the CEO subsequently decided to start another business in a completely different industry, taking him away from the marketing services company. To run the marketing services firm, he chose one of his sons to step in as CEO. While the son did have experience in the industry from working in the company, he had no experience as a CEO, or as any type of executive leader.

Succession planning is often a challenge, but nowhere is this need more profound than in family-owned businesses, where family, interpersonal, and organizational dynamics often impact the organization in ways not present in more mainstream company/ownership models. These factors often create resistance, create dysfunction, or present other barriers to healthy succession planning.

The son was well liked as the new CEO and had previously had a successful career in sales, but he lacked experience in the other skills necessary to run the company. After a relatively short period of time under his leadership, the company had become unprofitable and was in violation of several of its lending agreements. The founder, reluctant to remove his son from power, saw an opportunity to address these pressing issues and create a foundation for long-term success. He ultimately decided to bring in an Interim Executive to mentor the young CEO.

Working with the young CEO and the existing management team, the Interim assessed the situation and developed a plan that addressed several key issues:

1. The company was experiencing declining customer satisfaction and poor delivery efficiency/results. Customers were forced to deal with multiple departments within the company in order to successfully execute projects. This convoluted process resulted in inefficient delivery and very low customer satisfaction.
2. The organization was not structured for effectiveness, specifically there were a number of redundant functions across the multiple locations of the business.
3. The company was not stable. It had been unprofitable for some time, and cash reserves had reached levels where solvency was a concern, especially in light of violating its lending covenants.

A plan was developed that addressed these major needs by establishing a new organizational structure focused on creating a positive and efficient customer experience that was backed by streamlined delivery, requiring significantly fewer people. The resulting reduction in force led to immediate profitability and returned the company to compliance with lending covenants. The Interim CEO and permanent CFO then worked with the lenders to make sure the company had adequate capital moving forward. Once the company was healthy, the Interim worked with the founder and the CEO to develop a succession plan.

> The power of an Interim as an independent party should not be underestimated, especially in situations where emotions, history, and drama run high.

By facilitating a healthy succession discussion and planning process, the Interim helped the company reach the decision for the new CEO to become Chief Revenue Officer (CRO) and to recruit a permanent CEO. By using an Interim, the founder was able to address the company's issues, develop long-term strategies and plans for success and develop an appropriate succession plan that met everyone's needs. And the Interim CEO provided continuity of leadership as a permanent CEO was sought while the son moved to his long-term role as CRO.

The power of an Interim as an independent party should not be underestimated, especially in situations where emotions, history, and drama run high. Having an impartial facilitator who is laser-focused on defining goals and achieving success allows an organization make new progress on long-tenured issues. This is an incredible advantage of engaging Interim help.

BUSINESS IN CRISIS: TURNAROUND NEEDED

A national specialty retail company had grown very rapidly over the previous several years, but consistently lost money over that period due to massive cost overruns on expansion projects. Adding to the urgency of the situation, a large term note was coming due in a few months while the company also owed millions of dollars to contractors and vendors. The executive team that oversaw this growth to date was relatively inexperienced, and the company found itself in an existential liquidity crisis.

The board chose to fire the CEO and bring in an Interim CEO with extensive turnaround experience to initiate a twofold strategy. First, stabilize the company and establish a go-forward strategy that was appropriate to the specifics of the crisis. Then, with these pieces in place and transformation underway, recruit a successful permanent CEO with the necessary skills to execute the new strategy on a go-forward basis. The board desired this approach due to the speed with which a highly qualified Interim could begin. It knew that if the Interim selected was not able to produce results, replacing that person would be much easier than separating with a permanent CEO. Companies are often amazed not only by how quickly they can locate an Interim who can help their specific situations, but also the speed with which a quality Interim is able to start making meaningful changes within an organization.

The company clearly required additional capital, which was difficult to attract given the persistent losses, so the first cause of action was to shore up performance such that capital or funding could be sourced. The Interim CEO started by assessing overall top-line maximization and bottom-line optimization opportunities to improve company performance. In so doing, he identified some unhealthy organizational behaviors, concluding that the company was quite dysfunctional due to confused and muddled lines of authority, and a murky decision-making framework. Leading the charge and working with the existing management team and a cross-functional team of employees, the Interim created a plan to return the company immediately to profitability, largely through personnel reductions and the restructuring of the organization. As is often the case, the smaller organization was able to function much more effectively.

Once profitable, a comprehensive fundraising process was initiated that resulted in a number of reasonable offers for both mezzanine debt and equity investments. The most attractive investment was selected in time to pay off the term note, address past-due bills, and provide more than adequate working capital moving forward. With renewed stability and a go-forward strategy and model in place producing strong results, the company initiated a search for a permanent CEO with help from the Interim, ultimately finding a great long-term person for this position. These activities occurred over six months, erasing years of building challenges.

GRINDING GEARS: BROKEN BUSINESS PROCESSES

A successful direct-mail printing company was struggling

with profitability, operating at essentially breakeven although revenues were growing moderately and customer retention was reasonably high. The CEO and the board were struggling with how to improve profitability and realized that they lacked the requisite internal expertise. They agreed to hire an Interim COO with extensive experience in printing operations and, in particular, Six Sigma methodologies to instill discipline and commitment to quality practices.

Interims have the unique ability to bring very broad perspectives, experiences, and specialized approaches to their clients. This can be particularly true in established industries like direct mail where an Interim can add insights that have often been collected over decades of experience with established/legacy lines of business. It's surprising how techniques relegated to a lowest common denominator in a more modern and dynamic marketplace can still deliver solid results.

The Interim COO spent the first few weeks assessing the situation and developing options by speaking with customers and employees and by spending considerable time walking the shop and warehouse floors. He discovered the company utilized archaic and inefficient processes that required significant manual effort throughout the entire business. For example, a lack of accurate sales and operations planning resulted in needing to overstock raw materials inventory. And manual job scheduling resulted in production being assigned to less efficient presses, adding significant overtime costs.

Working with a team of key employees who had a deep understanding of the current processes, the Interim COO developed a plan to implement state-of-the-art systems for sales and operations planning, inventory control, and production scheduling. He quickly was able to identify the appropriate solutions and brought in a very experienced outside firm to implement them. As a result, the company was able to reduce inventory by 30 percent and overtime and overall staffing by 15 percent. EBITDA improved to over 15 percent from breakeven. The Interim's solid planning of all necessary components required to successfully complete this transformation ensured that existing employees were efficiently trained on the new equipment and supporting business processes.

With the new strategy in place and the company successfully executing, the company hired a permanent COO to continue executing the roadmap. The Interim helped facilitate a smooth transition of power.

> Interims approach assignments with a sense of urgency by focusing on execution and delivering fresh perspectives, subject matter expertise, and overall strong leadership.

COMPETITION INTERVENES: STRATEGY TO THE RESCUE

During the 1990s a very successful publicly traded distributor of technology products faced declining growth amid changing markets. Simply stated, its traditional ways of doing business had become outdated. The weakened company had traditionally sold its products through some physical locations and over the phone. The board and CEO accurately believed that the market was shifting to the growing e-commerce channel. Historically, the company was considered to be very astute at marketing, but it lacked the internal expertise to develop a new channel strategy to address the changing market. The CEO and CMO evaluated their options and decided to hire an Interim Director of Channel Strategy with extensive experience in channel development and, in particular, the growing e-commerce channel.

The Interim Channel Strategy Director initially spent time speaking with the customer-facing employees, particularly inbound sales, and to customers. He discovered that the company was very well regarded, offered quality products, and delivered excellent customer service. Nevertheless, some customers were shifting business to competitors because they had a superior online presence. He concluded that adding an e-commerce channel was critical to the ongoing success of the company but that it had to be done in a way that capitalized on the company's existing strengths.

Working with the CMO and the managers of customer service and inbound sales, the Interim focused on opportunities to maximize revenues. He led the effort to develop a strategy that added a state-of-the-art e-commerce presence integrated with the company's strengths through telephone support. The new approach allowed customers to research and even preorder products that could be immediately picked up at a local store. The company executed on this strategy under the Interim's leadership, accelerating growth and creating a strategy that many leading companies were adopting a decade later.

In this case and many others, Interims create long-term value that far outlives their direct involvement with a company, a notion that should always be top-of-mind for organizations considering the benefits of Interim leadership. Interims create immediate value by solving tough challenges and long-term value as these efforts deliver recurring benefits.

WHY ACQUISITIONS FAIL—INTEGRATION NEEDED

A rapidly growing software company made several acquisitions which successfully delivered on its goals of both acquiring new products and creating a larger and more diverse customer base. However, the company struggled to realize the value of these efforts as it experienced significant difficulty integrating the new products into its product line and higher-than-expected turnover in acquired customers and employees, a most troubling trend that was literally eroding the value of acquired properties daily.

According to the Harvard Business Review, many separate studies have shown that "somewhere between 70% and 90%" of acquisitions fail to meet pre-acquisition expectations.[6] The primary cause of these failures is poorly executed integration, which explains why Interims with experience integrating acquisitions tend to focus heavily on quantifying goals and identifying barriers up front.

The board directed the CEO to put a moratorium on additional acquisitions until it determined the cause of these issues. The CEO recommended engaging an Interim Corporate Development Officer (CDO) with experience in M&A integration to help. The Interim CDO would be engaged to triage issues with the recently completed acquisitions, to identify core challenges, and to develop a go-forward strategy for future successful acquisitions. One of the major investors in the company was a PE firm that had a previous relationship with an Interim CDO, increasing everyone's confidence in the decision. The Interim had some immediate availability, allowing him to start quickly.

The Interim CDO spoke to both current and former cus-

6 Clayton M. Christensen, Richard Alton, Curtis Rising, and Andrew Waldeck, "The Big Idea: The New MMA Playbook," *Harvard Business Review* (March 2011), https://hbr.org/2011/03/the-big-idea-the-new-ma-playbook.

tomers and employees. He met with the CEO and the board to get a better sense of their acquisition strategy and what each hoped to accomplish. He confirmed the core strategy of acquiring customers and new technology was sound, often yielding much quicker and more cost-effective results than de novo efforts. The Interim learned that once acquisitions were completed, the lack of integration planning resulted in customers leaving due to inadequate communication. A similar lack of planning resulted in poor employee retention.

Having solved similar challenges in the past, the Interim CDO developed a go-forward acquisition strategy, further refining the types of companies to be targeted. He also developed a detailed integration plan for potential acquisitions that focused on improving employee and customer communication, creating approaches designed to scale into the future.

With these plans in place, the board then authorized the next acquisition. The Interim CDO remained through the entire process and managed the post-acquisition integration using the plan he had developed. Throughout the process, he worked extensively and closely with existing staff, teaching them his tools and approaches, helping them understand the plan and support them in its implementation.

The next acquisition was considered to be very successful, realizing all major goals established at the onset. The Interim stepped out knowing that the company had the knowledge it needed to execute this plan going forward, and the company subsequently executed a number of successful acquisitions.

TRANSFORM OR DIE: COOL STUFF NOBODY WANTS

A highly publicized artificial intelligence company in the 1990s had burned through its initial investment with no marketable products to show for its efforts. The board, dominated by early investors, was growing impatient and decided to bring in an Interim CEO to assess the company's overall strategy and market opportunities relative to the technologies it had created. This approach was selected both for its speed and the board's desire for independent expertise to help it determine the direction of the company. Absent that, it felt it could not bring in an experienced permanent CEO for fear of continued losses. Once the search was started, an Interim was successfully located, deemed to be a solid fit and was ready to start within three months.

The Interim CEO was an experienced software industry executive. While the company felt it had developed very innovative technology and fueled its ongoing leading-edge development by hiring brilliant PhDs from leading universities, the Interim CEO quickly determined that the company misunderstood the basic definition of successful commercial innovation. The Interim educated the organization that success in the commercial space occurs not simply through the development of innovative technology, but rather when that technology becomes commercially viable by addressing a market need. Profits were necessary to sustain the company and fund research and new projects.

In attempting to maximize opportunities for sale of the intellectual property (IP) that had been developed, the Interim CEO discovered the notion of commercial success or addressing market-based needs was completely absent from the team's approaches to setting goals, assessing progress, and ultimately deciding what innovations to pursue. The company was caught in a trap familiar to many technology startups. Namely, developing technology that is interesting to the developers without any clear definition of how those innovations will generate meaningful revenue. The company was not rooted in solving marketplace problems or creating products/services that customers would be interested in actually buying.

Understanding this expectation gap, the Interim CEO held several extended sessions with all key members of the company to explore in more detail the features that made the technology unique and the options for commercial applications. The Interim brought in several industry experts with extensive knowledge of relevant markets to meet with the team and learn about the company's technology. Several unmet market needs that could be addressed by the features of the company's technology were identified during these sessions.

Although there was some disappointment in the team as the focus narrowed from green field research to practical product development, several promising products were identified that could be created from the team's work to date. Fueled by significant input from target customers, a product was developed and launched within six months, putting the company on track for long-term stability. This product became a leader in its niche, a position it retained for many years, creating team enthusiasm.

With new insights, the experience of a successful product launch behind it and a solid go-forward strategy, the company found and hired a permanent CEO with experience in the space. A few years later the company was successfully sold to a larger technology firm, gaining a significantly higher exit price and valuation multiple due to having substantial revenues and profits from its commercial successes.

SUMMARY

These case studies are representative of successful Interim engagements and demonstrate some of the many instances in which Interims help organizations. Interims approach assignments with a sense of urgency, focusing on execution and delivering fresh perspectives, subject matter expertise, and overall strong leadership. They confidently attack real challenges and opportunities, always keeping common goals in focus as they deliver results.

The value Interims create extends both through the end of an engagement when they typically help find and facilitate transition of important items to the permanent executive and well beyond their departure as organizations leverage the work accomplished as the basic long-term results.

CHAPTER 2

DEFINITION

INTERIMS ARE NOT TRADITIONAL CONSULTANTS

Consultants provide expert professional advice as outsiders, or nonpermanent employees of a company. Management consultants are those individuals who help companies through analysis of existing organizational problems, focusing their efforts on recommendations for improvement. Executives, on the other hand, are defined as individuals that have the power to put plans, actions, and laws into effect. They possess senior managerial responsibility in an organization. They are experienced leaders.

Interim Executives blend the skills of seasoned executives with approaches often used by high-performing consultants. Interims drive strategy, develop plans, and lead the execution of major transformational (*X-Formational*) initiatives, while serving as mentors and coaches to those around them. They are ultimately accountable to the organization for the results they deliver, and therefore have the full decision-making authority as the permanent executive in that position.

An additional area of crossover and overlap between Interims and other high-end professional service providers is in working to turn around failing companies. In many of these cases, consultants, as well as lawyers and accountants, are brought in to advise on these issues and execute tactical restructuring of the business (resolving balance sheet issues, restructuring debt, selling assets, and executing bankruptcy filings and plans). Here the distinction between Interims and consultants is similar, with Interims leading change through the turnaround, directing the actions of others while also adding value to the process through their experience.

EXECUTION

An important distinction between Interims and traditional consultants is the expectation of execution. As the famous UPS commercial mocking consultants says, "We don't actually do what we propose, we just propose it."[7] Interims may propose, but they always lead and do.

A hallmark of an experienced Interim is the ability to solve

7 Luis Castro, "Consultants," YouTube, May 2009, https://www.youtube.com/watch?v=P7M7A34b6Rw.

challenges and present practical approaches based on their real-world experiences solving similar problems for other companies. Interims develop strategies knowing that they will be leading the execution and will be accountable for their results based on the real value they create. Interims challenge theory and speak from experience, stressing realism and bringing skills to solve complex multidimensional problems. As a result of this experience, the strategies produced are typically more robust and grounded in reality than those developed by others with fewer, or no, expectations of leading execution.

Interims exhibit a bias toward action, focusing on speed over study, using experience and intuition as a guide. While studies can provide valuable data to confirm key assumptions and understand complex situations, this approach often requires extended periods of time. Much of what Interims are charged to accomplish must be done quickly, as delays exacerbate the issues being addressed, with a popular notion being to act quickly because most things are obvious. Driven by end results and urgency, a typical Interim will be accepting of, and prepared for, mistakes made during *X-Formation*, provided the team learns the cause and develops plans for never repeating the same mistake in the future.

LEADERSHIP

Interims lead organizations from within, utilizing many tools and approaches of high-end consultants, but they always exercise direct authority over employees who report to them as defined by organization/accountability charts. The act, and expectation, of direct leadership and decision-making is a clear differentiator between a consultant and an Interim.

> Interims are adept at turning strategy into plans and plans into action.

While some consultants are seasoned executives, Interims always are. Interims fill positions similar to, or often less senior to, positions they previously held at various points in their careers. Many Interims exhibit leadership through engagement, sharing their unique knowledge about the tools, techniques, and best practices with others in the company to engage those around them in problem-solving. Interims are adept at turning strategy into plans and plans into action, and in doing so teach others in the company to be execution-oriented and data-driven, creating better results.

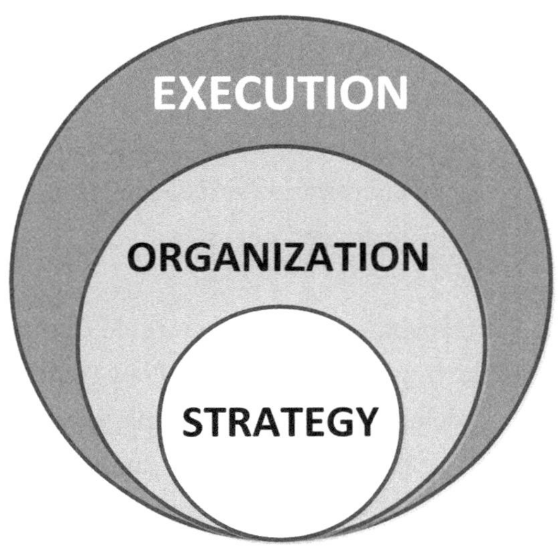

While bringing many of the same skills as a consultant, Interims bring considerable additional attributes, including leadership, management, mentorship, governance, decision-making and often take a much wider view of the full organization's needs. This diagram captures these key differences. Interims cover the entire domain while executive-level consultants often focus only on the inner (strategy) domain.

ACCOUNTABILITY

Another key difference between an Interim and a consultant is accountability. Interims, by definition, are executive-level leaders in an organization for a nonpermanent duration. As such, Interims are accountable to the organization to fill all of the functions defined for that executive seat, lead their team(s) and attain the results expected for their given area of the organization. This key difference should always be top-of-mind for an organization as it considers the best type of help specific to its defined needs.

Interims are transparent and accountable to their direct reports and the organization at large. They create accountability by practicing leadership and management, holding others responsible to them and to the organization. Interims hold other members of the executive team accountable in ways that others often do not. With no ties to past decisions, Interims honestly assess what is working and what is not without emotion or bias, speaking truth to power when they see issues that need to be addressed or opportunities that must be considered.

A seasoned Interim knows that wins are created by team efforts and that the first team that needs to be healthy and high-functioning in an organization is the executive team. Interims understand that their success will be limited by dysfunction and, as a result, they hold others at all levels of an organization accountable for their commitments and end results.

Interims often exhibit great skills in teaching others, a necessary quality in communicating and implementing change. This level of engagement with staff and peers typically creates increased awareness of the importance of accountability, and fosters team spirit. It raises the bar much higher, especially for companies that have struggled in the past to create a culture of self-management or attain stated goals. Accountability shines a bright light on the value each function contributes to the company.

> Interim Executives blend the skills of a seasoned executive with approaches often used by high-performing consultants. They drive strategy, develop plans, and lead execution of major transformational initiatives, while serving as mentors and coaches to those around them.

Case Study: Transformation Through Alignment

The printing industry has been faced with dramatic changes over the past several decades, some positive, some negative. E-books, online forms, and the overall move to digital media have negatively impacted many printing companies, resulting in stalled growth in these enterprises due to strategies and methods of execution that are now outdated.

One forms printing company had moved from slow growth to negative growth, marking the start of a potential death spiral if unchecked. It recognized that online alternatives such as electronic forms and other technologies were severely affecting revenue. The CEO and the board concluded that they needed an outside view and a broader perspective.

The company engaged an Interim Chief Marketing Officer (CMO) from the technology industry, a choice driven by the urgency of the situation and the speed with which an Interim could start helping. The company also saw a great deal of benefit in using an Interim to set strategy and lead execution up front, so that a permanent CMO could be found once the go-forward strategy was in place and producing positive results.

The Interim CMO started by assessing the overall health of the organization and, within two months, was able to identify two major driving issues that needed to be addressed:

1. A large, well known consulting firm had developed a strategy that split the business into three independent operating groups: forms, labels, and business process consulting. The consulting firm moved on, and the plan was implemented by the company with uneven results.

   The consultants had focused almost entirely on organizational structure, missing key needs of customers. The reality was that a majority of sales involved components of each of each of the three operating groups, and coordination of these complex orders was proving difficult under the new structure. The burden often fell to the customer to deal with multiple parts of the organization, resulting in dwindling customer satisfaction. Basic notions were often the topic of dispute, including which operating unit had ownership of key customers. The prestige of the consulting firm and the expense of the project made the CEO very reluctant to change. What looked like an elegant solution on paper became a disaster in execution.

2. The company was attempting to replace printing services with software, but had relatively little experience in the digital technologies that were threatening the base business. This strategy could not be successful for two main reasons. First, the company could never sell enough $99 software packages to replace million-dollar printing jobs. Second, the core competency of the company was the creative design of forms to address complex business processes, not software sales.

Fueled by data and insights from customer interviews, the Interim CMO worked with the CEO and other key members of the management team to implement the following plan to address the issues:

A. The organization was restructured using the Interim's experience and perspectives by reverting largely to the original structure but keeping some changes that had produced solid results. Under this plan, product management remained in the new structure, while manufacturing returned to a combined unit. Most importantly, a single team of account executives was created that represented all parts of the organization to each customer. The account executives became a single point of contact for the customers. The Interim CMO continued to work with key customers and the new organization throughout the transition to ensure its success.

B. Printing technology itself was also changing. The advent of full-color digital presses allowed high-end printing directly from digital files without the need to create the traditional physical printing plates used on offset presses. Working with the existing management team, the Interim CMO helped develop a business plan for a distributed real-time digital printing alternative to traditional offset printing. This new process enabled new products, building on the company's core competencies in printing and business process analysis. The company maximized revenues by implementing a very effective sales process utilizing the expertise of the existing sales force.

C. The plan required significant capital investment, which was approved by the board based on the large upside opportunity it represented. The board was compelled to action based on the Interim's complete vision and confidence in the plans he created to execute the changes. The opportunity for positive *X-Formation* became obvious. The new lines of business were launched within six months and immediately returned the company to growth. The existing management team was augmented with permanent executives appropriate to the new business. The success of the new business lines ultimately placed the company in a prime position to be acquired by a major competitor.

With the full authority to lead the company in strategy and execution, the Interim CMO was able to spearhead the bold *X-Formation* that was necessary for the company to survive by optimizing operations, organizing it for efficiency and maximizing revenues through new online channels.

SUMMARY

While much of what Interims do in practice is often similar to consulting, there are several major differences. The first is a focus on execution. Whether developing strategies and plans or executing them, Interims focus on getting results, valuing speed and action over study. Consultants sometimes have operating experience, but Interims always do. They bring advanced insights, experiences, and tools to bear while solving what are often urgent, and always important, business needs for their clients. Further, Interims are accountable to the organization for achieving complete results, which means that an Interim Executive has the same power, decision-making authority, and budgetary responsibility as would the permanent executive in that same seat.

CHAPTER 3

PEDIGREE

QUALITIES OF A SUCCESSFUL INTERIM

Companies looking to engage an Interim always have a lot on the line, with the company's strength, viability, profitability and scalability often hanging in the balance. An integral part of an Interim's value proposition is how well he or she can integrate into a company, assess complex and unfamiliar people/processes/technologies, define strategies to address the situation and execute the resulting initiatives. An Interim's ability to help a given organization, therefore, depends greatly on that person's experience, skillset, personality, and temperament.

Of course, the expectations of what an Interim will deliver can vary greatly from one company to the next and within each role. A large company navigating the choppy waters of bankruptcy, restructuring, or turnaround is likely to need a different set of skills than that of an early-stage startup seeking to raise capital, establish a first viable product, and place itself into a marketplace. Similarly, a company looking for an Interim Chief Information Officer (CIO) could have any of a nearly unlimited number of technology needs, including technical architecture, application development, solution design, business/technology requirements definition, information security, implementation or development frameworks, staff mentoring, and many more. No two Interims are alike, and no two roles are alike, requiring the right skillset to be matched with the right client.

Given the combination of high stakes, often unclear scope, and potential breadth of activities that typically need to be addressed, it is no wonder that companies often doubt how a temporary outsider to the organization could not only have a positive impact quickly, but also create lasting long-term value.

In fact, the action of hiring an Interim can feel unfamiliar and counterintuitive. After all, an Interim is not a consultant, although engaging an Interim often looks and feels like hiring a consultant. Further, the mainstream and long-standing definition of an executive is that of a permanent, full-time leader with authority to utilize company resources to accomplish sustainable results. Since consultants rarely have authority over budgets or to hire/fire employees, the mechanics of enabling an Interim can be befuddling for many companies.

Interims occupy a nontraditional spot as an outsider in the American corporate culture, namely leading the company in its entirety as CEO, or in another executive position, as a nonpermanent member of the executive team but with the full authority a permanent executive would wield. Many companies are unclear regarding their true needs and opportunities for improvement, which can further cloud thinking on the value an Interim could deliver. After all, how could anyone add value if we don't know what is needed?

So, if an Interim is a chameleon who is not employed by the company he or she leading, but is also not a consultant, and oftentimes is called upon to add expertise in several different parts of the organization, then what qualities should an organization look for in an Interim? And, how do you know if the Interim you're considering has the skills you'll need, especially if you are unclear on what those needs may be?

The remainder of this chapter outlines some key qualities Interims possess that allow them to be successful time and time again in creating both immediate and long-term value in these challenging roles. Chapter 10 goes on to discuss how a company can best assess fit and ultimately engage the right Interim to address its specific needs.

A PROVEN RECORD OF SUCCESS

Regardless of the company, circumstance, or assignment,

an Interim is hired to perform and is measured by totality of results delivered. While there is clearly a spectrum of roles and challenges that can come into play for a given assignment, quality Interims are hired to solve problems, and each brings a track record of successfully solving complex real-world problems many times over.

Successful Interims exude calm confidence in the face of real-world pressures and a constantly changing business landscape, demonstrating their extensive experience solving complex and unfamiliar problems within their domain of expertise. This steady approach is a manifestation of an inner calm that most seasoned Interims have in uncertain circumstances. Having been through many past extensive *X-Formations*, Interims tend to not be upset by unknowns, trusting their tried-and-true methods for helping each client capitalize on its unique opportunities. Given the uncertainty of change and the feeling of being overwhelmed, many clients are amazed at the calm confidence Interims provide. This calm comes from the past experiences converting daunting challenges into successful outcomes with other companies.

Interims tend to be data driven, evaluating options in the light of cost/benefit trade-offs. By employing successes from past assignments and sharing these experiences openly, Interims teach their executive peers and key employees how similar issues are solved by other companies, but never in a manner that would suggest personal boasting or score-keeping. Interims take assignments for the greater good for the client, not personal glory, realizing that accomplishments are the result of team efforts and not their brilliance.

Interims know that every situation requires their complete engagement and that they will be measured by their current, not past, accomplishments. Thus, they leverage successful habits and approaches repeatedly throughout their careers when the situation warrants.

SPECIALIZATION

While there are many qualities that set Interims apart, domain expertise may be the most important. Each engagement an Interim undertakes is a new adventure, with a large number of possible factors that need to be understood and acted upon in real time. So, deep knowledge in areas anticipated to be of the highest value, of the greatest risk, or of the most complexity is critical as an organization seeks to solve problems outside its abilities. All Interims hit the ground running with a strong base of knowledge in the job they are being asked to perform, focusing on those items that are unique to the client's business and looking for areas clearly out of phase with best practices in those disciplines.

Specialization manifests itself in the domain expertise an Interim exhibits in extensive knowledge or skill areas as well as specific industries or markets. While simple in concept, the domain expertise required to effectively solve the challenges of a given situation can be complicated, murky, and often in conflict with other areas of proficiency. For example, a company struggling with poor operational performance, could be suffering from bad processes, inadequate tools/data, deficient accountability/leadership or other maladies. Complex problems can often include a dizzying number of factors requiring use of hard skills such as proficiency in a given technology or methodology and soft skills like leadership, management, coaching, and culture building.

The best approach to understanding an Interim's capabilities in relation to an organization's needs is to break the facets down into their constituent parts, starting with the largest components, then getting more granular in areas of highest need, risk, or payback. Some common domain dimensions to consider include:

Industry and Niche—While no two companies are created alike or operate the same, it is important that an Interim have a solid foundation in the business an organization performs. For most organizations, this starts with the industry in which it operates and oftentimes extends to a specific niche. For example, e-commerce retail companies vary greatly from those in brick-and-mortar retail, requiring proficiency and skills in different disciplines. Any company considering engaging an Interim should be clear about its particular business model and hear from the Interim regarding how that Interim's experience maps to their specific needs.

Position and Title—Past experience in similar roles is critical to ensuring a good overall fit. While many Interims can (and do) fill many different types of roles in organizations, companies should start by qualifying candidates based on their past experience in that same position. Smaller companies may have needs for a single Interim that would typically span several roles at larger companies. For example, a fifty-person manufacturing company may have need for a seasoned COO to help scale its processes to address forecasted demand for products while also requiring supporting technology strategy that will allow it to start automating the simplest parts of its process today that will scale to support and ERP solution tomorrow. Smaller organizations often combine roles from ideally separate functions into a single executive job, with a common example being the Chief Sales Officer (CSO)/VP of Sales also owning Chief Marketing Officer (CMO) responsibilities until the company reaches scale. Regardless of the factors at play, any company looking to engage an Interim should ensure it is clear on the requirements of the position and the experience it feels is needed.

Company Size—It is important for companies and the Interims that serve them to understand the dynamics and requirements that shape executive roles. Small companies operate in ways that are significantly different than those that are larger. An Interim with experience at very large organizations with thousands of employees will likely have little understanding of what is required of an executive in the same role in a fifty-person organization. The same holds true for Interims with experience leading smaller organizations who step in to lead much larger companies. The political, administrative and functional modes of operation in very large companies can be very bureaucratic and dramatically different than the nimble methods and brisk pace of smaller organizations. Many Interims have experience at companies of varying size, but this factor should not be overlooked in vetting candidates. A useful tool in assessing fit is a day-in-the-life approach whereby the person engaging the Interim shares with prospective candidates typical tasks, challenges, and anticipated needs, allowing the candidate to articulate how he or she plans to be successful in the proposed role.

Context—Every company has specific factors that impact its need for quality executive leadership. These could include market dynamics influencing the company from outside, operational/financial/technical or other factors that influence the company from the inside. Or, more esoteric and confounding challenges, like politics, vision, culture, or related soft issues that impact the company in less direct means but which simply refuse to align with the rest of the organization. Similarly, a company looking for an Interim CMO to guide it through a disruptive product launch will need the steady hand of an experienced Interim who has successfully employed guerrilla marketing tactics and other nontraditional tools in the past. And certainly, a company looking to seize new market opportunities with an expectation of explosive growth will want to consider Interims who have demonstrated success in launching products, reinvigorating product lines, assessing the true performance of all products/services offered, and developing multifaceted sales and marketing plans.

Interims expect the client to have issues, dysfunction, and major challenges that require the help of a seasoned executive. Therefore, it is critical that an organization be honest with itself and clear on its most pressing needs and share these openly with any Interim being considered, regardless of the intended length of the engagement. Any company considering an Interim should clearly define the specifics of its situation, starting with immediate challenges, goals and constraints, then extending to short-, medium-, and long-term goals to provide context for why these things matter. Sweeping issues under the rug or scoping down due to uncertainty, dysfunction, or other limiting approaches should be abandoned when considering an Interim and when setting goals for the results that person will be called upon to deliver. Remember, at heart, Interims are change agents whose primary mission is to help their clients overcome thorny issues.

BIG BAG OF TRICKS

Companies looking for Interim Executive leadership often have a broad set of needs that can be difficult to quantify or ascribe to one specific role. Many companies considering Interim Executive assistance focus solely on the immediate pain points without full consideration of the breadth and scope of opportunities for improvement that the Interim will be asked to undertake once initial challenges are successfully addressed. This is natural as the fires that burn hottest in an organization are those that typically create the need for Interim help and are top-of-mind early in the process. But many companies are amazed at how quickly the right Interim can meaningfully solve stubborn problems that have become entrenched in the organization. Therefore, the opportunity for these companies is to take the full view of its needs, define the Interim's role clearly, and also identify other areas of the company that have needs where the Interim's experience and proven approaches can add value, without having direct oversight.

Section 2 details the manner in which Interims approach unique challenges to assess what is, and what is not, working by employing the *X-Formation* execution disciplines of strategize, optimize, maximize, and organize. These approaches are used to assess what is and is not working, to plan short and long-term approaches, to execute those plans, and ultimately to evaluate the results. This approach allows Interims to start making progress and adding value quickly, while keeping long-term needs in mind, creating a concentric circles approach that results in continual refinement and improvement after initial gains are created.

> Companies are amazed at how quickly the right Interim can meaningfully solve stubborn problems that have become entrenched in the organization.

Once primary goals are being accomplished, an Interim will then focus on the next level of improvement in processes, infrastructure, people, or other needs that are often overlooked at the onset of the engagement, knowing that the success of his or her tenure will be measured by the overall results delivered and not simply the initial set of activities. Experienced Interims typically employ diverse methods and utilize approaches they have successfully implemented elsewhere to measure performance and drive strong results. These include best practices, proven models, innovative technologies, tactics, and similar tools/approaches designed to deliver results, allowing companies break through to the next level of performance.

As the case study below illustrates, a great Interim will often lead the charge—when others are unwilling, unable, or have tried with poor results—by drawing on necessary skills and tools along the way.

Case Study: Reorg Redux—From Inventory Management to True Accountability

In 2015 an Interim CIO was hired by a consumer product goods company to serve in a fractional capacity two full-time days a week to help the company solve critical operational problems. This company desperately needed a new IT strategy and systems to set it up for explosive growth. This $8.5 million company was a market leader and had ever-growing demand for its popular products. Despite having a relatively simple sales model and channel strategy by only selling its goods wholesale to dealers, the company was experiencing order processing backlogs exceeding seventy-five days. The problem was intensified by an inventory accuracy of less than 70 percent.

The company was very savvy and had made many operational improvements as it grew over the previous eight years. When it was unable to solve its order processing and supply chain problems, it assumed it had made all of the process improvements that were possible, and now needed to invest in more technology. The Interim CIO was hired to help align the company's strategy with a technology plan and to add enabling technologies and processes to reduce order backlogs to less than thirty days and increase inventory accuracy to 95 percent or greater.

Shortly after starting, the Interim began evaluating the inventory management and order processing procedures with the staff. Processing an order required the involvement of three different groups: allocation/picking, packing/shipping, and inventory control. The latter was charged with monitoring each group's activities and solving inaccuracies which could be caused by any of the groups.

During his second week, the Interim went to the COO, asking to speak with the person who ultimately owned all of inventory accuracy. Three names were given in the context of different job functions that impacted inventory. Believing he had not been clear, the Interim again asked for the person who was ultimately responsible. Upon receiving the same answer, it became clear that there was no single person or group responsible, meaning no one was accountable, which clearly identified the issue. Further exacerbating the problem was the fact that all of these groups did not report up to the same part of the organization, often resulting in conflicting direction and approaches, and overall ineffective solutions. The resulting gridlock became a major barrier in permanently fixing the larger issues that frustrated the team, which felt it was taking proactive measures and could not understand why results were not improving.

At the next executive team meeting, the Interim CIO outlined the facts as he understood them, which were confirmed by the others in the room. He explained the issue in the context of the problems that are created by poor accountability and outlined some best practices in organizational alignment and structure. The Interim was a veteran of leading hierarchical, matrixed, and team-based companies. He had been a part of dozens of large and small company reorganizations during his time as an executive-level technology consultant to large companies and as an entrepreneur himself. To him, the opportunity for solving many problems with improved organizational structure and clear, nonoverlapping responsibilities was obvious.

Emotions ran high as the executive team came to realize that its company would need to be restructured to address and solve some of the underlying causes of the struggles the company was experiencing. This was an incredibly painful realization as the company had just completed a re-org six months prior. Regardless, the

Interim informed the team that its maximum order processing capacity for the current year was far below what it would need to meet the stated revenue goal. As he now understood the company's current operational capacity by assessing performance using hard data and supply chain modeling, the Interim showed the executive team that the absolute maximum sales volume the company could support with its current structure, processes, and performance would only support 75 percent of the stated sales goal. This realization caused the executive team to acknowledge that major steps would need to be taken immediately, with the Interim CIO leading the charge.

Despite the shock and disappointment of needing to restructure the company and the real risk of missing its sales goal for the year, the CIO led the team through exercises designed to create and test the new accountability chart. The executive team of nine was trimmed to six (another difficult decision). The operations group was organized around core functions, ceding total inventory control to a single group that oversaw all processes that affected inventory counts, all reporting to a new COO. Within three months, the company reorganized the distribution center personnel, implemented a more efficient layout, and refined its core processes, increasing order throughput 100 percent and raising inventory accuracy to 85 percent. Within another three months, Inventory accuracy increased to over 95 percent, and order processing backlog was reduced to less than thirty days. Six months after identifying this issue, the company was able to support 300 percent more transaction volume.

The Interim CIO worked with the head of sales to modify ordering and back-order management policies with an eye toward reducing shipping delays by focusing on in-stock items. He also collaborated with the head of production to refine order and supply chain processes and rationalize the product line with a focus on measuring the performance of every single product, instilling a mindset that every SKU has to earn its shelf inch. These further improvements combined to eventually reduce order processing backlogs to a mere three days and increase in-stock items dramatically by focusing on keeping best sellers in stock.

Supporting this increased performance required less staff due to improved efficiency, fewer errors requiring investigation/repair, and an optimized distribution center (DC) layout. Using these strategies and making other improvements, the company was able to grow 50 percent while reducing its staff by 30 percent over the next 18 months, focusing on profitability rather than hyper growth. The leaner company proved to be more focused as well.

At the end of the day, none of the changes recommended or implemented to solve these problems required any new or expanded technology, although they did require better use of the company's existing Enterprise Resource Planning (ERP) system. And likely none of the changes made would have been considered without the guidance of a seasoned Interim Executive who saw the company through fresh eyes, immediately recognized familiar challenges, and brought new perspectives and innovative approaches for solving stubborn challenges.

Great Interims spend time teaching executives and employees how to take their organizations to the next level and overcome challenges using proven approaches and strategies. Interims use these skills and proven tools to lead the charge, ensuring that the organization is learning new skills and gaining competency, not building long-term reliance on the Interim themselves.

ACTION-ORIENTED

Interims survive by delivering real results, in real time,

quickly. This imperative necessitates a sense of urgency in tackling all facets of executive leadership and can best be described as having a bias toward action. It cannot be stated enough that a quality Interim is not interested in a long-term role or parsing tasks out over a longer-than-necessary time frame to stay busy. Interims tend to charge a premium price for their activities, and along with that price comes a sense of urgency, with an expectation that the client will start seeing progress in areas of highest priority quickly. Lengthy studies, reports, and the like are not part of a quality Interim's approach as these activities do not add value quickly enough. It goes without saying that all executives should make decisions based on careful thought, hard data, assessment of options and risk, and the like. However, an Interim by nature exhibits these qualities and presents approaches that are designed to reach decision points thoroughly and quickly so that real problems can start to be solved.

In areas of primary accountability, an Interim will quickly assess the overall state of his or her department(s), prioritize items needing change, and produce an action plan aligned with the stated company goals in a manner that integrates well with activities in other areas of the company within defined budgets. An Interim wields the same authority as a permanent executive, and is empowered to make change within the defined bounds of that position.

For dysfunction extending beyond a given department or

discipline, Interims are typically the first to call out the elephant in the room, shining a bright light on issues others are hesitant to tackle. Typical culprits include political infighting, cultural malaise, poor accountability, weak business practices, poor enterprise performance, etc. Interims add value by rising above the issue at hand, creating a platform to bring leaders and key employees together to objectively discuss and resolve the core issue, and showing strong overall leadership in addressing potentially painful issues. Interims need to deliver major gains to their clients, and energy wasted on unhealthy endeavors can serve as a real barrier to success. Therefore, addressing these issues early and proactively is an imperative for Interims.

This third-party approach to addressing issues at the top of an organization often has a calming and cleansing effect, especially for parties that have been locked in conflict and see each other as unreasonable or uninformed. Interims are trusted advisors who practice their craft at the top of companies. As a result, other members of the leadership team are often willing to let go of past constraints, trusting the Interim can guide them to better results based on experience. Seasoned Interims bring practical experiences backed by solid results, working from knowledge and experience and not theory or conjecture, allowing the team to cover new and productive ground.

CHANGE AGENT

To say that Interims come prepared to lead change for their clients is an understatement, as these high-performing individuals expect change and challenges and need these items in their diet. Their ability to see opportunity through change and transformation is their collective reason for being and is exhibited in some of the following ways:

> **Entering the Danger**—This is a common rallying cry and personality attribute of many Interims. Simply put, this is the quality of being fearless in entering unknown situations, openly calling out weak decisions that should be revisited (in a healthy way), and generally committing to driving complex issues and challenges to conclusion with few knowns. Great leadership teams sometimes lack the skills, tools, or proper perspectives to tackle tough issues as a company grows and faces new challenges.
>
> As problems grow in size and complexity, leadership teams often shrink back, fearful to make additional mistakes which may create additional problems or place the executives involved at risk. Once effective decision-making on these large and important items stalls, the cycle stalls, and dysfunction accelerates as large issues/needs/opportunities pile up.
>
> Using proven approaches and their vast experience leading through difficult circumstances, Interims become

accustomed to confidently leading organizations despite having limited facts and experience with a particular company. Regardless of the factors involved, Interims always face danger head-on, as complete results cannot happen otherwise.

Fresh Perspectives—The entrance of an Interim to an organization creates the opportunity to honestly assess previous decisions, plans, and commitments. Through fresh eyes, Interims will speak truth to power, identifying areas that do not ring true to them based on their experience helping many other companies oftentimes by asking simple questions designed to assemble all of the pieces of the organization's puzzle into a go-forward vision. Often, leadership teams fall short of solving complex problems, not because of a lack of effort, intelligence, or having the best intentions. Rather, they simply lack the specific skills or experience to solve very large, complex, and often highly specific problems holistically.

Innovative insights and honesty coming from someone with broad experience, a track record of success, and no personally vested long-term interest in the outcome (aside from helping the company reach its goals) can be freeing to a company and its leaders. Approaching stubborn problems from new directions allows areas of misalignment, poor definition, or simply poor strategy to be readdressed in positive ways. Interims are typically viewed by an executive team as an opportunity to gain quality executive guidance and reset many items that are not fully working. Simply stated, an Interim has no ties to past plans or decisions and is focused 100 percent on addressing current challenges, even if painful, with real solutions to create a compelling go-forward plan.

Apolitical—Organizational politics, grandstanding, power plays, end runs, and other forms of poor corporate behavior are real barriers to the effectiveness of organizations and the Interims that serve them. With no long-term stake in the organization, Interims can navigate areas that may be too treacherous for others. Regardless of the political makeup of any client, a quality Interim conducts business in an open and honest way that is transparent to all and leaves politics aside. Quality Interims are simply too busy addressing the real needs of a client to waste time on organizational politics or turf wars. As one Interim puts it, "Taking bullets comes with the territory and is part of the value I deliver!"

> Interims use proven approaches and their vast experience to confidently lead companies through difficult circumstances despite having limited facts and experience with a particular company.

GREAT FACILITATOR

Interims enter unfamiliar surroundings needing to gather facts, identify perceptions, and realities and ultimately lead the organization forward to new and higher ground. Therefore, many Interims possess and utilize excellent facilitation skills to create common understanding of strengths, issues, opportunities, and options. While arguably not required, this skill tends to be present in most experienced Interims as a practical matter. In fact, many Interims will be called into new companies for standalone facilitated sessions designed to achieve a specific goal, such as creating a one- or five-year strategy. Companies feeling misalignment should specifically inquire as to an Interim's experience facilitating company-wide reorganization, as these skills will likely be required to bring together a team of leaders who have grown hardened in their opinions and approaches.

GRACE UNDER PRESSURE

An Interim's world is one in which change is constant. This is particularly true during engagements in which the client is trying to solve very large problems or take advantage of significant opportunities that the organization has not been historically adept at solving. The nature of these assignments requires a strong leader with a calm temperament who expects bumps along the way. Experienced Interims confidently build plans and calmly adjust those plans as inevitable challenges emerge, expecting some surprises as they lead teams through often unfamiliar *X-Formation* endeavors to ultimate success.

Remember, an Interim is a temporary leader in a company whose interests are in helping the client solve problems in a healthy way so that he or she can be replaced by a permanent executive. An Interim is not a traditional consultant! Interims have skin in the game in that they stake their reputation on the success of each and every client. They experience and lead large-scale change daily and are resilient, exhibiting confidence and grace under fire. Their conviction and certainty in action creates a calming effect with other leaders and the company at large.

THIRD-PARTY CREDENTIALS

Interims, by nature, tend to be individual contributors. This can make it challenging to assess not only the specific skills the person possesses, but also whether or not the Interim is of quality. Chapter 10 provides a deep and insightful look into how an organization can assess the fit of a given Interim to its needs. Aside from assessing these specifics, companies can look to independent or third-party means of assessing an Interim's quality and experience.

> InterimExecs knows firsthand that excellent consulting or executive skills alone are not enough for someone to be an outstanding Interim.

The first and most meaningful way to assess an Interim's current strength and viability is to vet that person's membership in the Association of Interim Executives, or InterimExecs as it is now known. This organization has been independently assessing the skills of Interims since 2012, setting the bar quite high for admittance to its membership ranks.

InterimExecs carefully screens all applicants, evaluating their past documented Interim experience. It requires applicants to have a minimum of three true Interim assignments, each demonstrating transformational real-world results. Meeting this standard is critically important as many individuals present themselves as Interims when they have not yet proven that they can tackle the full depth and breadth of skills required to deliver results in these challenging roles.

InterimExecs knows from firsthand experience that excellent consulting or executive skills alone are not enough for someone to become an Interim. Based on its tough real-world assessment, this high-quality association rejects 98 percent of applicants. For companies looking for the best-of-the-best, InterimExecs has a further, premium designation: RED Team. The RED Team, short for Rapid Executive Deployment, is comprised of truly standout performers who can be deployed quickly in urgent situations. They often work as a team to assess the company and put in place immediate action plans designed to address critical needs where the company's survival is immediately at risk.

Aside from association membership, active and quality Interims tend to have other tangible artifacts created through their work and passion. These items may include Interim-focused writings (blog posts, published articles, or books), or other accreditation(s) that are germane to the skills that the Interim utilizes, including Six Sigma or certification in methodologies which that Interim routinely puts to use.

SUMMARY

Any organization looking to solve complex problems, attain new heights, or address deeply embedded core issues should start by being clear on the full scope of its needs. It should ensure that any Interim who is considered has relevant experience and possesses specific skills the company feels are needed for success.

Accomplished Interims are well-rounded leaders who exhibit a broad set of complementary skills, backed by extensive real-world experience. They remain calm in the face of uncertainty with an innate ability to tackle the toughest challenges. Interims are results-oriented individuals whose stated accomplishments can be verified through third-party corroboration, as the success of every engagement is necessary for them to remain viable.

CHAPTER 4

VALUE NOW!

THE ECONOMICS OF INTERIM ENGAGEMENTS

All organizations periodically have the need for additional executive horsepower due to the sudden exit of a key manager, transitional issues, acquisition integration, crises, or needed organizational change. When the organization does not have someone available or qualified to assign to the area of opportunity, Interims step in to help—always with a focus on the value that they can help create. Value is created when positive benefits delivered exceed the costs required to create those results (money, time, effort, and lost opportunities), with the most powerful investments being those that create benefits that extend far into the future and that greatly exceed all costs.

The notion of using Interims as high-value corporate tools

is well established in Europe and is starting to become more commonplace in North America. Interims tend to be expensive by traditional consulting standards, with rates typically ranging from $300–$700 per hour. In considering the costs of an Interim, companies should always bear in mind than an Interim is not a typical or run-of-the-mill executive. Rather, most Interims have extensive experience that would require many careers to assemble. For example, one Interim reported leading major *X-Formational* initiatives successfully with forty separate companies over a fifteen-year period. Clearly, the population of individuals with this scope of experience is very small.

Therefore, the value an organization can derive from an Interim's help should not be obscured by that person's hourly rate or total costs. Rather, value should be measured based on the results that will be delivered as compared to the actual costs. For some companies, the stakes (and required value) are so high that equity or profit sharing is included in the agreement in addition to the hourly rate, travel expenses, etc. This fact alone shows the incredible transformational power an Interim can affect in critical situations and also the magnitude of results a company should expect when engaging that person.

Interims create a great deal of value for their clients, often surpassing up-front expectations. Knowing that the cost of transforming a company and addressing mission critical needs will be substantial, organizations looking to engage an Interim should focus on the overall value proposition of that engagement/relationship first, ensuring that the costs are within the company's means and balanced with the anticipated value in both the short- and long-term. Examining the costs or risks of inaction is as equally effective as identifying benefits and opportunities in gaining clarity on the importance of an Interim's involvement.

It is for these reasons that the following factors, in addition to dollars that will be spent, should be considered when determining the value that will ideally be created for the company, its investors, and its employees when engaging the help of an Interim.

TIME IS MONEY

For fast-moving companies, the notion of time is an important one. This is especially true for those under extreme pressure to resolve major issues or to get to the next level. Many seasoned Interims share experiences of having companies pass on their services, deciding to tackle challenges internally, only to be asked back for further discussion months or years later when the company was unsuccessful in making meaningful long-term progress. These companies gain an appreciation for, and often lament, the costs of lost time.

Interims focus on making meaningful progress and creating tangible results daily. They understand the time value of money and bring a number of key characteristics to the engagement, using these techniques (and more) to create value rapidly:

- Interims are often available almost immediately and can be in place much quicker than a permanent executive and many other types of consultants.
- Interims are specialists at dropping into a crisis situation, being effective from day one.
- Interims bring domain expertise, enabling them to address problems in their entirety by using proven approaches and by creating better results.
- Interims deliver tangible results quickly by clearly separating short- and long-term needs and by focusing on items of quickest return.
- Interims teach, mentor, and coach executive teams and companies in general in best practices and new tools and techniques. These aspects of an assignment create lasting value for executive teams as they adopt more sound approaches and develop cohesive relationships.
- Interims lead by example, modeling great communication techniques and demonstrating transparency to bring the team together.
- Interims maintain high professional standards, remaining focused on the task at hand, skillfully avoiding productivity traps such as politics, in-fighting, or drama.

- Interims typically use agreements with short termination notices, allowing the organization to move quickly to its new stable state once the Interim has completed the major goals of the assignment. Interims understand this dynamic and proactively plan for a smooth exit when the time comes.

TOTALITY OF RESULTS

Executing swiftly only creates value if the end results are sound. Interims, through their deep and varied experiences, often approach challenges in unique and expansive ways. Having resolved many complex problems in challenging circumstances at companies across different industries, an Interim will typically apply best practices and past successful approaches to help clients define solutions that can be realistically implemented within constraints defined. The result is a much more comprehensive, strategic, and realistic solution that addresses immediate pains while also building a base for long-term success. It is quite common for organizations that have engaged Interims to use the work products, strategies and approaches created during the Interim's tenure for years into the future.

Additionally, many Interims create value for a likely client even before beginning an assignment by detailing exactly how they would approach solving the challenges presented, the results that should be expected and their assessment of the time and effort required. Some Interim engagements start with a small piece of assessment work up front (typically two to six weeks) to help the company more clearly understand its needs and the specific approaches the Interim will use. These paid assessments are valuable to both parties, clarifying challenges and opportunities and creating a valuable work product the company can use, whether it engages the Interim long-term or goes in a different direction. This approach is especially useful for any company that feels it needs to work more on problem-solving before seeking Interim help or that may fear wasting an Interim's time or overpaying for easy fixes.

It always should be remembered that quality Interims are quietly confident when entering situations with a large number of conflicting factors, unknowns, and risks. They use their past experiences and successes to create a unique, specialized approach based on any client's specific needs.

POLITICS BE DAMNED—LET'S GET TO WORK

Politics are the enemy of efficiency and represent real barriers to performance and attainment of results, often shielding underperforming parts of an organization from the bright light of visibility and accountability. Interims know that time is money and are respectful of, but not encumbered by, company politics or culture. This allows them to move quickly and question openly. They bring new perspectives and focus on the immediate issues without biases from previous strategies, slaying sacred cows in the pursuit of solid and holistic strategies and plans.

While Interims will review the history of how the organization came to its current predicament, they tend to be driven by facts, hard data, clear plans, and true accountability. Using information they collect to present an independent analysis of the current issues and their ramifications, Interims use an outside perspective to present unbiased findings and solutions to the current management team, creating renewed focus on what matters most.

In addition to a focus on resolving issues immediately, completely, and efficiently, Interims bring significant skill in presenting data and solutions, collective enemies of politics. Typical consulting engagements culminate in the presentation of findings and recommendations, often in the form of a series of large binders. Interims, on the other hand, quickly assess data, present options for moving forward, and foster team collaboration to reach consensus by demonstrating quality leadership. When members of the leadership team, lost in the fog of war, drag their feet or resist change to the detriment of necessary progress, Interims know how to listen, coach, and influence to make progress and course corrections as needed.

SMART MONEY USES INTERIMS TO MULTIPLY RETURNS

Perhaps one of the strongest endorsements for the value created by the Interim Executive model is the one made by private investors, VCs, and other institutions that represent smart money. These organizations and individuals frequently cultivate networks of Interims as a strategy to make rapid gains, establish clear vision, and address major challenges as they make more permanent changes to the executive team of companies they control. Interim Executive leadership is a tool used by sophisticated investors to realize their goals and create expected returns.

With a forward-looking view focused on producing the highest returns possible, savvy investors typically seek out companies with the potential to spark change, produce growth, or fix what is broken. Fund managers strive to be in the business of transformation, providing money along with solid, experienced leadership to help take a company to the next level. For these results-oriented organizations and individuals, that change must be exponential, not incremental.

"We look for situations where we can actually bring some operational expertise to the table," explains one investment banker. "We look for a business where we know before we buy that we could do X, Y, and Z to improve the operations of the company and get a return for our investors."

Bringing in operational expertise can come in many different forms and in all deal stages from pre-acquisition to revenue growth optimization to company exit. Smart and savvy investors know how to utilize Interim talent when needed, including in the following scenarios:

PRE-ACQUISITION

Investors know that a bad investment is deadly, and to ensure they are getting the best bang for their buck, they will often utilize the skills of an Interim to perform due diligence on a potential investment. Interims typically possess a broad array of specific skills that enable many to assess the business operations, financials, markets, technology stack, competition, and other critical aspects of a potential acquisition. In many cases the fund or private investor will engage the Interim to take an active role within the company, develop a growth strategy, or execute a turnaround plan, or execute other changes to get the company on the right trajectory.

MAXIMIZE REVENUE AND GROWTH

Investors also call on Interims when legacy leadership does not have the right skillset or when guidance from a veteran executive is needed to align with the company's strategy with the fund's vision.

The leadership that can take a company from startup to

$20 million may not be the same team to lead it from $20 million to $50 million, and so on. As Marshall Goldsmith so famously wrote in *What Got You Here Will Not Get You There*,[8] each major revenue tier creates new challenges that test an organization's ability to scale and forces it to invent new and better ways of doing business.

One principal at a $415 million Florida-based fund that works with many founders of family owned companies has experienced these challenges firsthand. An existing VP finance or controller, for example, may never have worked with a parent company or major investor and may require guidance to start using best-in-class financial reporting. This principal observed, "If you said, 'Close the books faster, convert the financials to GAAP, and manage the debt structure' their head might explode!" As a result, the act of engaging an Interim CFO "is by far the biggest 'no-regret' move" for this high-performing fund.

To scale a company or optimize growth for a future bigger sale, Private Equity (PE) and Venture Capital (VC) firms will draw on outside expertise to tackle all areas, including revenue generation, cash conversion, process and supply chain optimization, product development, sales training and forecasting, brand positioning, technology and systems, and governance or leadership practices.

8 Marshall Goldsmith and Mark Reiter, *What Got You Here Won't Get You There: How Successful People Become Even More Successful*, Revised ed. (New York: Hachette Books, 2007).

These sophisticated investors also seek Interim help when they find themselves in unforeseen situations, such as when a key executive has a health crisis, family emergency, or other matter that forces that person to leave the job suddenly. In these instances using an Interim allows for quick action designed to establish continuity of leadership, buying the company time to evaluate if the executive will return. The interim model scales well to situations with major unknowns and provides ongoing leadership while the company searches for a permanent replacement should the permanent executive not return.

Companies facing a sudden unplanned executive vacancy most often do not have the luxury of doing a thorough search for a permanent replacement, which can takes many months impede overall company progress. Interims can jump in within days to lead a company, stabilize the situation, and define the go-forward plan.

EXIT

A textbook use for an Interim is in helping a company prepare for an exit. Selling the company, preparing for an IPO, and merging with or acquiring another business are classic and well-established uses for Interim Executive leadership, where expert help can create exponential results. Companies often discover opportunities to significantly raise the asking price by correcting issues that are reducing revenue or profits, or that can position the company for a higher exit valuation multiple. Interims, as on-demand executives, fit well in these scenarios as goals are clear and urgency in action is necessary.

Interims many times are viewed as deal specialists who tackle known needs and test stated strengths to prepare the company for optimal valuation. Some common areas of need include preparing accurate and detailed financials, developing forecasts or models, enhancing business plans, and optimizing product roadmaps for target acquirers. Specifically, Interims working to attain positive exit scenarios tend to focus on the *X-Formation* disciplines of optimization and maximization, creating the healthiest possible bottom line and largest top line. These activities create the greatest corporate valuation, thus the highest exit multiple.

In the case of merger or acquisition, an investor cannot risk the companies not integrating well. The integration process is vital, as the anticipated value of acquiring a new company can quickly dissipate as the number of complex items that need to be assessed and properly addressed can balloon, slowing progress and limiting opportunities. Interims specializing in these activities will tackle needs broadly, as each area of poor integration will reduce overall return on investment and enterprise value. In the case of family-owned businesses, Interims often take active roles in the succession planning process, helping a company prepare for multigenerational exit, taking the opportunity to cash out the legacy leadership team as the next generation comes to power. Interims involved in facilitating these transitions work alongside and mentor the next generation of executive talent as transition occurs.

IT COMES DOWN TO ROI

Owners and boards view Return on Investment (ROI) holistically, taking into account short- and long-term costs and returns. This view extends to the costs of, and results provided by, Interim Executives. For one, Interims do not come with the added costs of a permanent employee, such as paid vacation days, health and insurance benefits, and severance or pension payments. Interims also provide none of the complexities of traditional executive employment, creating maximum flexibility for the client as it sorts through long-term options.

Second, the time it takes an Interim to get up to speed is minimal. On day one, a typical Interim will start the assessment process, gathering as much information as possible to understand the current situation and most pressing needs or greatest opportunities. As soon as the picture emerges, go-forward plans are created, with execution starting shortly thereafter. Interims can be hired in days as opposed to the months companies spend searching for a full-time hire, which often equates to lost time and missed opportunity.

Most of the ROI delivered by an Interim will come in the form of tangible results, with many benefits extending well beyond the Interim's term with the company. A few examples of benefits that create a payback well into the future are a next-generation strategy, operations built to scale efficiently, sales and marketing tools designed to generate new sources of profitable revenue, and improved organization structure engineered to create proper alignment and maximum returns on people assets.

Interims also provide maximum flexibility, being able to scale services up or down as the company's needs demand. While Interims may begin full-on to complete a project or initiative, as they put process in place and empower the people around them, companies sometimes choose to scale back their time into a more part-time or fractional role. Many Interims ultimately ascend to the board of directors to create ongoing, long-term value.

With the flexibility and focus on results, companies and investors are increasingly looking to Interims to provide highly specialized leadership talent to help them solve big challenges, capture unrealized opportunity when change needs to happen fast, and, when desired, prepare the company for a quick and graceful exit.

COST TRADES

While seemingly obvious, it should not be forgotten that the costs of engaging an Interim need to be viewed in net terms, deducing cost trades or offsets. For example, an Interim occupying an executive seat is presumably offsetting the cost of a permanent executive in that role. Permanent employees' loaded costs are substantially higher than their base salaries due to benefits, bonus, profit sharing, equity, and payroll taxes. An Interim typically brings none of these costs.

In assessing cost trades and the true costs of engaging an Interim, companies should remember that Interims often work fractionally, occupying a role on a less-than-full-time basis. Many Interims work primarily in a fractional capacity, devoting one, two, or three days a week to a given client and having multiple client engagements under way at any given time.

Fractional Interim leadership has a couple of key benefits. First, the cost on a weekly basis (as compared to hourly) may seem more reasonable and comfortable. Secondly, and more importantly, full-time Interims can exhaust the capacity of their clients to absorb change and put new concepts to use. It can, therefore, be beneficial for all to utilize a fractional (part-time) Interim to even out demands on the team and allow time for new concepts to sink in and change to take root. It is also quite typical for Interims to introduce new notions that then require research or other offline planning by the executive team and organization at large. Working fractionally allows companies to use off cycles to undertake these activities. Using an Interim for two days a week, for example, reduces the cost significantly as compared to a full-time role, creating the opportunity to trade the fully loaded cost of a permanent executive for a part-time Interim.

Finally, Interims leave when the assignment is over. As compared with the complications of making a change with a permanent executive, changing an Interim's role is much more simple and rapid. For example, a company facing the exit of a permanent executive often incurs long lead times associated with human resources procedures, negotiation of exit/termination agreements, assembly of a severance package, and other complicated processes. Further, the time to locate a replacement once the seat is available is significantly longer with more significant stakes at risk when making a permanent hire. Interims leave with as little as several days' notice, expecting the transition far in advance as they accomplish their objectives.

Case Study: Shuttered Operations to Record Profits in Twelve Weeks

After two years of unrelenting decline and $6 million in losses, the owners of a packaging manufacturing company for table grapes decided they needed to bring in outside help to turn things around. The company was founded in 1973 by a group of grape growers who came together to produce boxes for their farming operations in the central valley of California. While manufacturing was not originally in the company's DNA, the business got to the point of creating a consistent product and quickly grew along with the grape industry.

That was until 2014 when things started to go sideways. "The company was somewhat in disarray," said one of the owners. "Our management team at the time was not working up to par, and there were some surprises in year-end numbers." By 2015, the company was in dire straits. It had gone from an anticipated profit to a multimillion dollar loss. There were problems with everything from bookkeeping to operations. When the company attempted to ramp up for the grape season, issues with several processes and broken machinery led to a plant shutdown. The company was at a complete standstill.

In crisis, the owners huddled in order to make hard decisions. While some felt the company should be shut down, others wanted to move forward with another approach: notching up the level of the executive team.

"We knew we needed to make a change, we couldn't continue to operate the way things were going at the time. I didn't have the skills needed to make that change, and once I recognized that, I knew we had to look outside to find someone who had those skills," said the CEO. He began to search for a lifeline and discovered InterimExecs' Rapid Executive Deployment Program, which matches companies with Interim Executive talent. After a call to assess the company's specific situation and needs, InterimExecs introduced the company to a veteran Interim with operational and turnaround experience across a wide range of industries.

After a phone conversation, the grape packaging company decided to move forward, and the Interim agreed to take on the assignment. The company ownership was optimistic. "We had a great feeling right from the start. The Interim is a capable, steady hand. Based on his background, we felt he was more than capable to take on the assignment, and we were relieved that we felt we had someone who was up to the task of turning us around."

The Interim CEO hit the ground running and quickly got the full picture of what was really going on. In addition to an inoperable plant, water waste was thirty-five thousand gallons per day in the midst of a severe California drought. The grape harvest was starting in eight weeks, and only twenty employees remained on hand, while over 150 were required for manufacturing.

Knowing he had to move fast, the Interim CEO began with an assessment of the company. This provided him with a full picture of the situation and allowed him to develop a plan, ensure the team was on the same page moving forward, and set expectations as to additional expertise or money needed to complete the turnaround to the ownership group.

"It's never clear from the start," said the Interim. "The people who are involved as owners and investors are not necessarily in touch with day-to-day operations, so you are getting background that may not be consistent with what your initial expectations were walking in."

With no revenue (due to suspended operations), the Interim looked to maximization strategies designed to land customers and generate orders to fuel the restart of operations. Orders would have to be delivered within weeks of the start of the harvest. "If we couldn't deliver in eight weeks, we were already behind the curve," said the Interim.

After assessing the company, the Interim CEO set out milestones to be achieved and presented them to the board:

- Return company to manufacturing before the harvest
- Return company to profits and positive cash flow
- Eliminate water waste
- Increase production output
- Increase quality
- Reduce overhead expenses
- Reduce product cost

The owners and board met to discuss the recommendations and the investment they were making in the Interim CEO. "It's not an inexpensive hire," the prior permanent CEO said, "but we felt it was worth it given the level of problems we had uncovered that needed someone of high caliber. We trusted that it would end up paying for itself."

The board gave the green light to move forward, and

execution started immediately, amazing the company ownership. The Interim took the reins, and progress was made within the first few months. The client was impressed with the amount of work the temporary CEO was able to get done and the amount of leadership he demonstrated, something that had been lacking from the previous management.

The Interim built confidence with the team using active listening to gain insights and repeated important topics back to ensure he was hearing the points correctly. "An Interim does not tell people what is going to be done. They ask people what they see that represents areas of concern. Many of the people have been doing these things for years. They may not have the perfect answer, but they have been watching and see what is successful," he said.

The Interim CEO immediately went to work to bring in outside resources, including filters on flatbed trailers to make sure the water was acceptable to the boiler, which at the time was strewn in pieces on the factory floor. He then encouraged the internal team to tackle issues around setting up production, testing quality levels of their resins and chemicals, fixing machinery, and laying out cost and a plan of action to meet the eight-week deadline. "He believed that the expertise was already here, but that people at the top level were not listening," explained the company's production manager.

These moves produced the following results:

- Highest daily/weekly production volume in company history
- Product costs reduced by 20 percent and continuing to improve
- Initiated capital investment program to repair, upgrade machines/molds
- Installed a new water well, and now recycle water with zero waste water
- Reduced overhead by 31 percent
- Established first preventative maintenance program for plant and equipment
- Increased prices and decreased delivery costs

From substantial losses in 2014 and 2015, the company became profitable within twelve weeks of the Interim coming on board. In addition to getting operations up and running, the Interim's positive leadership started to transform the culture. More cooperation and a new focus on quality over quantity, created increased employee enthusiasm, and participating in the solutions energized the team.

The client confidently stated that the Interim delivered a huge long-term value to the company, far exceeding the fees paid. In fact, it is now executing on a new strategy made possible by the transformation and entering new markets confidently, continuing to use the Interim CEO in an ongoing role as a trusted advisor.

SUMMARY

Organizations facing immediate and critical issues can greatly benefit from an Interim who will bring fact-based analyses of the business, a bias for action and approaches designed to create value quickly. While an Interim may cost more than the day rate of the outgoing executive or a more traditional consultant, companies should focus on the anticipated value that will be created, including long-term benefits it expects to realize. In looking at the costs of Interim Leadership, companies are often surprised to see that the difference between the fully loaded costs of a permanent executive and the Interim's fee are marginal.

Interims are prepared to start on short notice, are accustomed to becoming productive quickly, and are ready to leave on short notice. Further, Interims typically possess skills and knowledge that is often not present in an organization, allowing the company to attain outcomes that might otherwise be impossible for a given leadership team. These dynamics allow companies to maximize their return on the investment they make in transformational Interim Executive leadership.

SECTION 2

IT'S ALL ABOUT RESULTS

Interims are often misunderstood in two major ways, particularly in the US. The first fallacy is that an Interim is a placeholder, occupying a spot that was held by a true leader who had to vacate for some reason without a ready replacement. A lapdog, if you will. The second is that an Interim works like a consultant, assessing weaknesses, doing studies and creating proposals. To the contrary, Interims are experts at transforming organizations, leading companies through difficult challenges to new opportunities by executing with strength and clarity of mission.

Interims most often are engaged during a period of change at an organization. This change could be expanding into new geographies, launching new lines of business, reengineering to capitalize on unique opportunities, resolving bankruptcy, performing acquisition or privatization, breaking through important barriers (sales, operational and financial), addressing problems with accountability or culture, or diving into other large-scale problems. The common thread is that Interims are typically involved in leading companies through challenges that must be solved to survive and thrive.

> Interims are experts at transforming organizations, leading companies through difficult challenges to new opportunities by executing with strength and clarity of mission.

Since the stakes are always high, Interims come prepared to get started by quickly assessing the health of a company's major functions, working cooperatively with others at all levels of the organization to understand the full reality of the situation, and developing action plans designed to deliver the highest return in the shortest amount of time. Items requiring further investigation due to high cost, risk, or complexities are reviewed for the next steps required to break down the constituent parts.

As the truism states, "Execution eats strategy for lunch." This is particularly true for Interims as their success depends on being able to quickly assess challenges in unfamiliar surroundings to create solid action plans. The needs of a typical organization can be broken down into four major areas, each of which Interims approach from the perspective of execution. The following diagram illustrates the four *X-Formation* execution disciplines that Interims practice to transform companies.

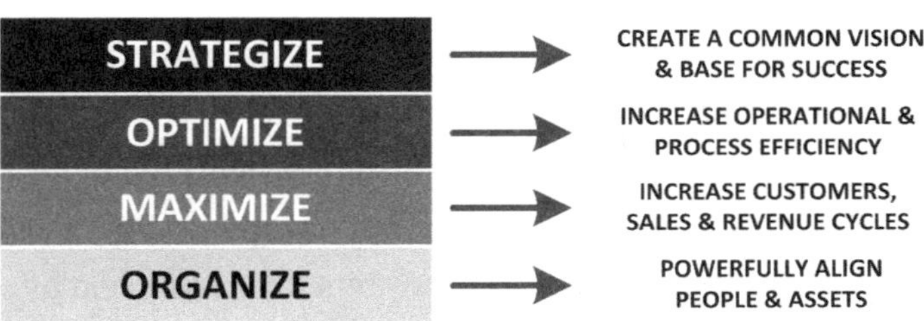

Interim Executive X-Formation Disciplines

Section 2 elaborates on what is meant by execution in these four key disciplines:

> **Strategize.** Volumes have been written on strategy and strategy development, but what is often neglected in the discussion is execution. Strong strategy forms the basis of transformation, creating a clear vision for the company. While execution trumps strategy in the abstract, executional excellence starts with sound strategy. Chapter 5 focuses on developing and executing strategy.

> **Optimize.** Optimization drives efficiency and reduces below-the-line expenses to increase bottom line performance. Chapter 6 focuses on approaches Interim executives use to help organizations optimize their

operations by eliminating redundancy and inefficiency through process assessment and innovation. These activities are ideally performed before ramping up transaction volumes, building a solid base for quality delivery and creating the ability for the organization to scale smoothly.

Maximize. Maximization efforts are focused on driving sales and increasing bottom line performance through growth of the top line. Maximization yields the highest return to an organization after optimization has occurred by creating more transaction volume to be served by a more efficient operation. Chapter 7 focuses on the ways in which Interim Executives help organizations address barriers to revenue growth.

Organize. The key to fulfilling the three objectives outlined above is aligning all resources in a company (people, equipment, physical plant, products/materials, and other major assets) around the strategy and core processes. Chapter 8 outlines approaches Interims employ to organize these assets, properly aligning all major resources around strategy and plans.

Within each of these disciplines, Interims tend to start with assessment of the current state. Once understood, plans are built to address the largest challenges and opportunities. With plans in place, execution is undertaken to convert plans into action and, ultimately, results. Once execution is started, the process is repeated to achieve next-level results.

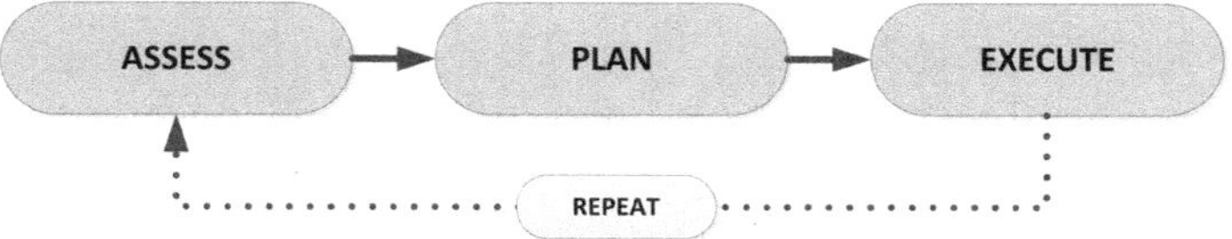

APE Framework: Assess, Plan, and Execute

Upon completing this section, you will understand how Interims practice the four execution disciplines to prioritize needs and use a framework designed to Assess, Plan, and Execute (APE), repeatedly revising approaches based on the client's most pressing needs.

CHAPTER 5

STRATEGIZE

CREATE CLEAR VISION, THEN EXECUTE

Great organizations often struggle due to the limitations of their thinking or approaches. The existing leadership team may fail to plan, develop, execute, measure, and refine plans as the company grows ever larger, faces the tough headwinds of a competitive marketplace, or battles stagnation in a business-as-usual approach. These challenges strain leadership teams, causing dysfunction, including analysis paralysis or buck-passing as the team contemplates the required large-scale changes and the very high stakes on the table. The longer this cycle continues, the harder change becomes as needs stack on top of one another, creating a logjam.

Interims help companies overcome these challenges by assuming either top-spot (CEO) or other C-level leadership positions over business functions in need of leadership and change. A company trying to solve revenue and sales problems would typically engage an Interim Chief Marketing or Sales Officer (CMO/CSO). A consumer products company with a quality or throughput problem would likely benefit from an Interim Chief Operations Officer (COO) or perhaps a Chief Technology Officer (CTO). A company battling bankruptcy or turnaround after devastating financial performance almost always can benefit from an experienced Interim Chief Financial Officer (CFO) or CEO. In the face of the difficulties of an increasingly complex Human Resources (HR) landscape, many companies are realizing huge value from engaging a fractional Chief Human Resources Officer (CHRO) or VP HR.

While all organizations utilizing Interims expect quality execution, what is often overlooked or undervalued is the ability of Interims to develop comprehensive strategies either for the company at large or for specific business units, products, or services. Interims often approach the discipline of strategy and planning differently from traditional consultants, knowing that they will most certainly be called upon to successfully execute on a strategy once complete. As has been mentioned throughout this book, one of the main differences between Interims and consultants is following through on the recommendations, always having the expectation of leading execution to ensure success, and not simply making recommendations.

ASSESS STRATEGY

The Interim's first job is to assess the largest needs of the organization or department, and this typically begins with a review of the company's strategy. Lasting operational excellence and revenue maximization result when sales, operations, finance, and other core processes are driven by a powerful strategy that creates a clear vision for the company.

A common corporate fallacy is believing that great strategy alone will produce exceptional results. Interims approach execution with strategy in mind and with the perspective of realistic execution. Success is a result of great execution, backed by an excellent strategy.

In general, strategy is more of a journey than a destination. Great companies set goals at different intervals with clear expectations for what will be achieved at each stage. For example, many great companies meet annually to reset their one-year strategy and also meet quarterly to turn that strategy into action. This approach ensures that the organization is constantly reviewing strategies and revising their specific plans as the environment changes and the effectiveness of previous plans are measured. This process is shown below.

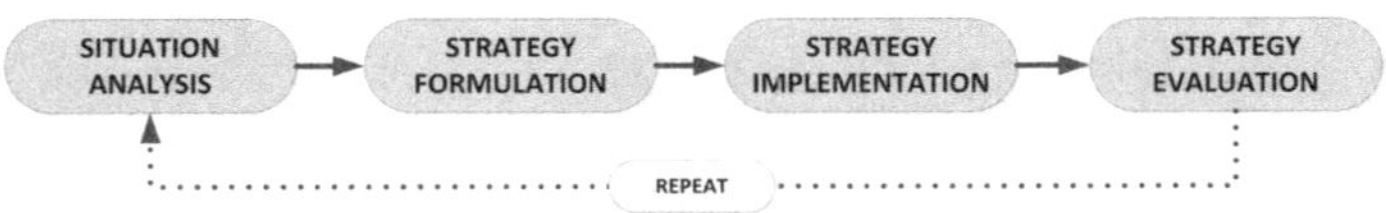

Strategy Development Cycle

Interims bring with them not just substantial experience in strategy development, but also unique perspectives gained by repeatedly stepping into organizations and by seeing the real-world challenges that arise in translating vision into plans and converting plans into actions. Some key reasons that Interims cite for the failure of strategies to deliver expected results include:

> **Does Not Capitalize on Core Competencies**—While counterintuitive, it is not uncommon for a company to lose sight of what makes it special, how it creates unique value for its customers, or how it ousts competitors with powerful operational processes, a company's special sauce, if you will. Sometimes this is because the company never had a tight grasp or full understanding of these advantages. However, most often this result occurs when a company loses focus as its organization and operating model grow more complex due to increased sales, products, services, and more complicated approaches. Interims help a client evaluate and rediscover its unique abilities, sharpening strategy around these core strengths, not only because these are areas of past success, but also because working within a core competency provides the greatest leverage and biggest opportunities for larger and more powerful returns.
>
> **Lack of Resources**—Even a well-crafted strategy will fail if the company is unwilling to dedicate adequate resources

to the *X-Formation* effort in the form of time, people, and funding. Quality Interims know there is no point in building or executing plans that are based on poor (or undefined) resource assumptions. Interims use their experience to build models to assess if the strategy contains a realistic estimate of all resources required up front to prepare the organization for these investments and to test that the proposed benefits greatly outweigh the fully loaded costs. When resources are scarce, they spearhead discussions designed to clarify the highest priorities, largest needs, and opportunities for greatest payback.

Inability to Move Quickly with Quality—Larger organizations are often inherently slow to implement new strategies while small organizations are, on the other hand, prone to failures from moving too quickly. Organizations of all sizes frequently struggle to maintain quality while pressing the limits of available capacity. Since Interims work to both help companies achieve scale and also turn those that are struggling around, they benefit from having used a large number of tried and true tools and approaches. Past tools are deployed as required on subsequent engagements to maximize speed of execution while increasing quality of execution. These proven processes further reduce uncertainty and risk as the Interim can share firsthand experiences from similar situations and incorporate past lessons learned into the strategy.

Lack of Change Management—Interims, free from many of the encumbrances that saddle employees of a company, are often able to see radically different end states than can be imagined by the company's permanent leadership. A core competency of Interims is expertise in leading companies through the large-scale changes required to execute a new strategy with excellence. Change is present in all their assignments, so Interims become experts at identifying changes that need to be addressed (and barriers that need to be removed) to go from the present to a future state. Change management involves the skills and activities required to proactively assess the current state of a company and define the gaps that exist between the strategy and company's current people, process and technology capabilities. Success in identifying and managing these anticipated impacts is critical to the success of all major undertakings, and many smaller ones as well.

Poor Execution—Overall poor execution, which may be the result of any of the above issues, is the single biggest cause of strategy failure. For companies that struggle with execution, Interims will often suggest, and help implement, tools and proven frameworks designed to deliver specific results. Common frameworks and tools such as the Entrepreneurial Operating System/EOS®, Scaling Up© and Khorus can help organizations establish clear vision and provide an ongoing framework for excellent execution. Regardless of the tools utilized, Interims are task masters who lead execution and manage their direct reports in executing well-crafted plans, ultimately holding themselves and those on their teams accountable for end results. Executing the wrong strategy can be as damaging as not executing any stated strategy, so Interims further use tools designed to ensure that any changes to strategy are assessed fully to understand likely impacts to endeavors already underway.

Even if an organization is committed to defining and executing a great strategy, many companies struggle to quantify results or to know if strategy is sound. In a 2010 Harvard Business Review article, Robert Simons outlines seven key questions each company should ask itself in reviewing its current strategy.[9] These are:

1. Who is your primary customer?
2. How do your core values prioritize shareholders, employees, and customers?
3. What critical performance variables are you tracking?
4. What strategic boundaries have you set?
5. How are you generating creative tension?
6. How committed are your employees to helping one another?

9 Robert Simons, "Stress Test Your Strategy: The Seven Questions to Ask," *Harvard Business Review* (November 2010). https://hbr.org/2010/11/stress-test-your-strategy-the-7-questions-to-ask?referral=00060.

7. What strategic uncertainties keep you awake at night?

Interims ask questions like these to facilitate discussion related to strategy and tactics, looking for problem areas where vision is unclear or in conflict with other stated goals and where large gaps between the company's capabilities and goals.

PLAN CHANGES

Plans convert strategy to action. And a strategy without a corresponding plan is a fallacy. Interims sometimes step into companies that have a solid and well-considered strategy but that are struggling to convert that strategy into tangible results. In these scenarios, as well as in efforts to convert newly defined strategies into action, Interims will look at the whole picture to create plans that include all major components necessary for success. These include:

> **Goals and Objectives**—Strategy provides the broad strokes and orients the company around large concepts that will ideally drive all aspects of execution for a stated duration or the foreseeable future. Powerful strategies impact the entirety of an organization, meaning that multiple plans are created to address all of the needed transformations company-wide. The first step in translating this into a plan is to clearly state the goals and objectives of each plan. Goals ideally are set outlining revenue growth, expense reduction, capital raise, or

other measurable criteria. Stating goals simply promotes transparency and clarity, creating a baseline for measuring results and sharpening the team's focus on items of importance. Goals can also be stated in terms of major accomplishments that may not have a financial metric, such as, "Transition main manufacturing line to new facility by May 31."

Scope—Scope establishes the bounds for activities to be undertaken in a project or task. Scoping is critical to success, especially for complex initiatives. Generally speaking, high-level scoping is sufficient for major transformations. For example, in planning to revitalize a product line, scope would be established by stating any products/services outside of the scope of the plan and why. The goal of setting scope is to provide the team clarity on areas to be included in the transformation and those that are not, eliminating distractions and maximizing efficiency. One experienced Interim CIO/CTO, observed that many IT project failures are due to poor scope definition, which resulted in unclear operating parameters and exponential complexity. Continually adding large unplanned components late in these struggling initiatives created constant change, eventually resulting in failure. This seasoned Interim remarked that in virtually all of these failed initiatives, it was never the technology that failed outright, but rather lack of business scope and goals that wreaked the havoc.

Budget—A budget should be created for all major undertakings, even for must-have transformations that have seemingly obvious benefits to the company. Ideally, budgets should be as detailed as possible, segregating expenses from asset investments and clearly delineating cash out the door versus any financing or other fundraising upon which the plan relies. Major capital projects should always have a capitalization/depreciation and tax plan and assumptions stated to ensure a major financial setback does not hamper transformation efforts. Knowing that improperly funded plans is a leading cause of failure, Interims (regardless of the seat they occupy) often lead the budgeting discussion.

Resources—Clear definition of resources required to be successful is necessary for all significant projects. Major transformations typically occur real-time while the company is still executing its legacy model, which can result in over allocation of key resources and conflicting priorities. By developing strategies with an expectation of leading any subsequent plans, Interims test assumptions, call out anticipated conflicts and help their clients make sometimes difficult decisions regarding go-forward activities to ensure realistic goals are set. Once clear, plans are confidently developed, and resources are efficiently allocated.

Communication—*X-Formation* is generally driven by

new and innovative ideas for how a company should do business. This process, or even its notion, can terrify employees at all levels of an organization. The planning phase is designed to turn strategy into action. Once actions are defined, clear communication becomes as critical to overall success as the details themselves in creating alignment and positive energy around *X-Formation* plans, as well as allowing employees to ask questions or present concerns. Most Interims have many stories of improperly, ill-timed or flat-out incorrect messaging that was delivered by a client which placed the overall initiative at risk. Such major gaffs can threaten great strategies and plans by disenfranchising employees, damaging morale, and drawing energy and focus away from the important work that will need to be done to realize the new vision. It should always be remembered that communication plans need to be developed for both internal and external audiences, created well, and delivered properly to achieve maximum alignment.

Issues and Impacts—As basic as it sounds, any large issues or impacts (good or bad) should be specifically stated as part of any plan. Plans tie together the execution aspects of strategy, creating a common reference point for what is to be accomplished. Therefore, any known knock-on impacts or issues that need to be dealt with should be stated up front, minimizing surprises. Interims are forced to solve problems that often have many facets, or dimensions. Backed with lots of experience identifying and resolving complex issues, Interims burrow into challenges to facilitate a complete discussion of factors at play and anticipated impacts, often uncovering many more items to be considered than initially presented. This approach is necessary to mitigate overall risk to the initiative and surprises along the way.

Phasing—Many companies view strategy and supporting plans as an all-or-nothing proposition, whereas Interims tend to see many potentially fruitful paths. They are seasoned veterans of projects and large-scale transformations that took too long or required too many resources to deliver meaningful results. As a result, Interims often facilitate discussions to explore must haves and phasing changes with a focus on creating as much value for the organization as quickly as possible. Proper phasing allows the company and leadership team to keep all efforts focused on current goals, using early phases to create tangible wins while setting the stage for later and typically more complex actions. All phased plans should state current and future goals clearly, and show how each part fits into the whole.

EXECUTE STRATEGIC TRANSFORMATION

Helping companies formulate solid strategy is a common need that Interims fill. In fact, it is not uncommon for companies to reengage with past Interims for quarterly or annual strategy sessions following the primary assignment, which makes sense given the deep knowledge and insights Interims gain while working with their clients. Executing a transformation in strategy requires complete and careful forethought of all components that need to be defined before executing large-scale changes designed to accomplish the new vision for the company. In leading efforts related to transforming the strategy and making it execution-ready, Interims use some of the following tools:

Situation Analysis—This includes evaluating all of the factors, both internal and external, that an organization currently faces. A number of frameworks exist that can help organizations through this process. These include environmental scans and audits, SWOT (Strengths/Weaknesses/Opportunities/Threats) analysis, internal reviews, market research, customer interviews, employee interviews, and others. External factors are often analyzed using frameworks such as Michael Porter's Five Forces, which considers industry competition and the bargaining power of customers and suppliers, as well as how the threat of new entrants or substitute products may impact a company.[10]

Strategy Development—Once the current situation is

10 Michael E. Porter, "How Competitive Forces Shape Strategy." *Harvard Business Review* 59, no. 2 (May 1979): 137–145.

well understood, appropriate strategies can be developed. Interestingly, many times by simply making a few key decisions, other components of the vision become self-evident. Interims often facilitate this exercise, or contribute a heavy voice throughout, as they generally have been through this process many more times than their permanent executive counterparts. To achieve continued and ongoing success, Interims have to be successful throughout the entire *X-Formation*, causing them to forward-engineer plans, anticipate challenges, and provide insight into the effort that will likely be required. By presenting challenges likely to be encountered several steps down the road, Interims help the leadership team foresee likely barriers up front, resulting in more realistic goals.

Strategy formulation is guided by the situation analysis and includes three main types of strategies:

- Functional Strategies (operational)
- Competitive Strategies (business line)
- Corporate Strategies (guiding principles by which all efforts are aligned)

Metrics—Key components of any good strategy are well-identified and measurable metrics against which the success can be gauged. Interims tend to operate primarily on facts and data, often represented in the form of a scorecard or dashboard. By facilitating the definition of key business metrics, Interims help the Executive Team hone in on the most meaningful business drivers. In the early stages, the team can often agree on what should be measured, despite having no way of deriving a metric, spawning subprojects to gather data or otherwise measure results. These business measurements, backed by hard data, represent a critical final step in measuring current performance as the company prepares to convert a powerful new strategy into action.

Strategy Facilitation—Many organizations struggle to define the components that need to be included in their vision and strategy. Interims often provide not only valuable insights into a business, but also fresh ways of looking at opportunities, serving as catalysts for new ideas, and introducing proven practices to their clients. Proven approaches, when applied to a new opportunity, provide both the effect of empowering the company with a new direction, and minimizing the overall risk associated with the change due to past positive results.

The following are examples of traditional strategies that Interims may introduce based on the factors they see:

- Diversification
- Product line expansion, consolidation, or elimination
- Horizontal or vertical integration

- Retrenchment
- Acquisition
- Geographic expansion
- Recapitalization
- Operational/process improvement
- Outsourcing

CHANGE MANAGEMENT

Most organizations have a natural resistance to change, and *X-Formational* initiatives create a tremendous amount of change. Lack of change management is, more often than not, the key contributor to strategy failure. Since the presence of an Interim can be in itself a significant disruptor, the opportunity exists for each company and leadership team to adopt a change-oriented mindset, whereby other changes in the business can serve as a catalyst to fresh thinking and risk taking within acceptable bounds. Interims deal with change in virtually every engagement, so experienced Interims have well-developed skills to harness its power for positive results. For those in the organization who struggle to embrace change, resistance often manifests itself in some of the following ways:

- Desire to maintain the status quo
- Misunderstanding the reasons for change
- Fear of the future
- Concerns about job security

- Lack of sponsorship/alignment with organizational objectives
- Lack of resources to effect change
- Unwillingness to participate in change process
- Presenting general, rather than specific, objections to proposed changes

In presenting sometimes far-reaching visions, Interims are experienced in change management. Resistance to change is difficult to overcome, so Interims paint a vivid picture of the expected end state and its benefits, as well as any trade-offs to a sometimes-skeptical audience. Interestingly, change executed effectively often has a very positive impact on the organization. Knowing this, Interims tend to be natural cheerleaders by expressing realistic optimism for the future who remind the company at large of what is not working and needs to be addressed.

> Most organizations have a natural resistance to change, and X-Formational initiatives create a tremendous amount of change.

Change management is a structured approach to transitioning individuals, teams, and the organization as a whole from its current state to a desired future state. These activities require significant planning and proper discipline to build confidence and set the stage for success. Typical steps in this process include:

- Understand where the organization is at the moment.
- Understand where the organization wants to be. Determine when, why, and what the measures of success will be.
- Plan development in support of future goals in appropriate, achievable and measurable stages.
- Manage the process of implementing major changes in technology, business processes, organizational structures, and job assignments to reduce the risks and costs of change, and to optimize its benefits.
- Arrange for support during change for people within the organization.
- Communicate goals and plans clearly, facilitating involvement from people as early, openly, and fully as possible.

Case Study: Poor Product Strategy, Catastrophic Performance

A publicly traded supply chain software company was facing a crisis. The company was experiencing rapidly declining revenue, persistent losses, and a pending liquidity crisis. It had burned through virtually all of the cash it had raised through a public offering over the past five years. The crisis forced the board to remove the CEO and CFO. The search for a new CEO was believed to require too much time, and the condition of the company made the position relatively unattractive to top candidates. The board, therefore, decided to engage an Interim CEO to quickly identify and address the issues.

It became clear to the Interim CEO after speaking with employees and key customers that, for a variety of reasons, the company was adrift and needed a new strategy. Complicating matters, an open revolt was brewing among the customers. Most customers were Fortune 100 companies with complex supply-chain challenges. Many, if not most, were looking to replace the company's products with those from competitors, and several had filed, or were threatening to file, lawsuits. Publicly available customer satisfaction measures placed the company at or near the bottom of the industry. The following root causes were identified:

1. While substantial amounts of capital had been invested in product development, these efforts were focused on exploring new architectures and not developing enhancements desired by customers. In fact, virtually no customer input was sought, and customers saw no viable upgrade path to address their concerns.
2. Virtually no interaction with customer decision-makers was taking place. This exacerbated the view that there was no path forward with the company's products.
3. Day-to-day customer service was viewed within the company largely as an annoyance. Customer issues were left unresolved for extended periods.

Working with a cross-functional team of key employees, the Interim CEO developed a new organization structure focused on resolving customer issues. A knowledgeable senior employee was assigned to each key customer. That employee and the Interim CEO visited every customer. The new organization was empowered to mobilize the company's resources to resolve issues immediately. At the same time, the company refocused product development on features critical to customer success, and the new architectures were abandoned. The importance of customer satisfaction was reinforced throughout the company in order to shift the culture.

As a result of these changes, the liquidity crisis was averted, revenue growth was restored, and the company became profitable. The company was then able to recruit a very accomplished permanent CEO.

John Kotter's 1995 article in the *Harvard Business Review*, "Why Transformation Efforts Fail," outlines an excellent approach to ensuring successful change.[11] These are:

> **Establish a Sense of Urgency.** Once a course of action is chosen, move quickly, as windows of opportunity often close as quickly as they open. Urgency should not be misconstrued as the need to rush or act hastily. Rather, urgency should instill motivation and a sense of purpose in each person to work quickly but with quality and eliminating wasted or inefficient cycles.
>
> **Create the Guiding Coalition.** Transformation plans should be built by involving employees from

all parts and in all levels of an organization. The goal is to address the inevitable differences between the formal and the informal organization structure proactively and positively. This may be the single most important concept.

The first benefit of creating a guiding coalition is that the plans developed are based on all information available in the organization. The second, and most important, benefit is that it creates a ready-made group of advocates for change who are well respected and exist throughout the organization. These advocates become role models for the required behaviors as well as advocates for others when inevitable challenges emerge.

Develop a Vision and Strategy. A compelling vision vividly paints the goals for the organization, ideally backed by an equally compelling strategy. These combine to powerfully describe to the organization what the effort is intended to accomplish.

Communicate the Change Vision. Having a compelling vision is different than communicating this vision. Many organizations fail in sharing the vision in a meaningful way or with too few individuals.

Frequently communicating the planned changes in positive ways through as many channels as possible constitutes a best practice used by Interims to win the hearts and minds of those who will be helping to execute the transformation.

Empower Broad-based Action. Accomplishing major transformation is made easier when everyone in the company is charged with continuous improvement. Empowering and encouraging employees to find opportunities in systems and procedures needed to support the change helps create a proactive mindset and leverages the abilities of a larger base than top-down driven approaches. Obstacles to change need to be removed. Everyone needs to be encouraged to take appropriate risks.

Generate Short-term Wins. Short-term wins are too often hastily dismissed in the planning process as being too small or otherwise inconsequential. Interims measure any value that can be delivered early as being worthwhile and are often advocates for knocking down a few small goals quickly. Not only does this approach create forward momentum and some value to the company, but it also creates a feeling of success with those performing this important work. Interims consciously plan for and accomplish some successes as soon as possible, but also repeat the process throughout the engagement to fight stagnation or complacency. It is also important to note that many organizations have needs that change quickly. By breaking a larger goal into a series of smaller goals, the organization can make progress and cement results sooner rather than later, allowing it to be nimble as new needs arise.

Consolidate Gains and Produce More Change. Once an organization embarks on a transformational initiative, that initial change (or series of changes) has a way of breeding both the need for more change and an increased appetite for change as positive effects of previous changes create a stronger, more cohesive company. As changes manifest, Interims are always on the lookout for consolidation opportunities that allow for second- and third-tier innovations that build on earlier changes. This approach is critical to ensure that the resultant organization is fully optimized around new, better, and more integrated processes. More change is also required to address or eliminate less successful efforts that inevitably occur along the way. Interims show the company how to encourage and recognize change agents as thought leaders in new ways of doing business.

Anchor New Approaches in the Culture. Anchoring gains and developing long-term habits, procedures, and processes that support repeatable excellence are critically important in any type of transformation. Interims ensure the organization makes the complete transformation to maximize results, continually communicating the connection between these new positive behaviors and improved organizational performance. By celebrating *X-Formation* wins and capturing progress with scorecards, documented procedures, and other supporting practices, renewed culture and winning attitudes take root.

SUMMARY

Great strategies often fail as a result of poor execution, and at the same time, great execution cannot save a truly poor strategy. Interims work as agents of change, routinely finding themselves at the center of *X-Formational* activities for their clients. With much at stake at every engagement, they first help their clients identify strategy limitations prior to commencing assessment of optimization, maximization, or organization opportunities.

---

11 John Kotter, "Why transformation efforts fail," *Harvard Business Review* (March-April 1995): 59–67.

As the go-forward strategy becomes clearer, activities turn to testing assumptions, defining measurement criteria, and assessing the overall cost and effort of proposed changes. Interims convert strategy to plans by focusing on approaches that maximize near-term value, properly phase large-scale transformation, and ultimately are deemed reasonable and attainable by the organization. Extensive experience translating strategies into actionable plans enables Interims to confidently lead executive teams through this entire process. These disciplines serve an Interim well regardless of whether that person is leading enterprise-wide change as an Interim CEO or Interim president, or to individual units if working as head of a major business unit.

CHAPTER 6

OPTIMIZE

BELOW THE LINE INNOVATION

Optimization efforts strive to gain the highest return for the lowest cost on all company expenses. By looking first at costs related to major business processes, areas of potentially dramatic improvement can sometimes be quickly identified through small savings on a potentially large number of transactions. For instance, increasing the bottom line by reducing rent is good, but gaining similar savings on an operational improvement is better as a more efficient process will provide exponential payback over time as volume increases. And reducing rent has a limited benefit to any other parts of the business, whereas process innovation is often the catalyst for improvement of other, related processes. Therefore Interims concentrate not only on return on investment, but also on return on expenses and enablement of dependent processes, starting with the largest volume drivers and working backward from there.

Interims are action-oriented leaders. Unique in the depth and breadth of experience they bring to each assignment, career Interims look for ways to deliver real results to the clients from day one. To accomplish this mission, Interims use proven approaches to assess the operational performance/efficiency of business units and core processes. This examination reveals hidden value trapped within existing products, processes, and systems. Once these limitations and bottlenecks are understood, plans are developed to focus on the areas that can be transformed most quickly and those that will yield the largest return on investment. This chapter outlines how Interims optimize companies, driving efficiency and bottom-line performance.

ASSESS OPERATIONAL EFFECTIVENESS

Bottom line performance is directly correlated to an organization's efficiency and the quality of the underlying processes. Assessing optimization opportunities boils down to understanding a few key areas, then digging deeper in areas where cost is disproportionate with the amount of value added, or any areas where costs are outside of established norms:

Profits—The ultimate indicator of general health. Profits, or lack thereof, frame the overall size of the *X-Formation* opportunity, establishing the appropriate level of plan urgency.

Processes—Processes organize human and automated capital to produce a result. The costs of people and core processes is often large, difficult to calculate, or both. Process optimization and innovation provide payback on each cycle executed and set new baselines for ongoing improvement, delivering greater returns as volume grows.

Systems—Systems and technology are integral parts of virtually every modern business process. Inefficient, inadequate, overly expensive, or improperly utilized technology often presents large opportunities for improvement both in lowering actual costs and also lowering unit costs by processing more volume on lowered total costs.

People—The fully loaded cost of an employee must be assessed against the value that person in that role creates. Comparatively high employee costs often point to process or system inefficiencies, or to an underperforming employee base. As the largest single expense line item in many companies, Interims look to match employee costs to specific transactions as a means of finding the highest labor cost activities and opportunities to get higher return on labor dollars.

Raw Materials—Gross margin analysis shows the overall health of products. For most products, raw materials comprise the majority of the cost, so even small improvements in the cost of raw materials/parts can provide a meaningful payback when realized on every unit produced.

Overhead or Fixed Expenses—These costs are the total "nut" a company has to cover (net of the items listed above). Overhead is often overlooked in assessing opportunities for improved bottom-line performance, as these costs are considered difficult or impossible to change. Optimization of these expenses typically provides a one-time benefit without further opportunities for continual improvement or exponential payback, but which can still be meaningful in benefit.

Discretionary Expenses—It is amazing how discretionary costs become rooted in a business once they enter without much examination. Budgeting appropriately for Items such as travel; food, beverages, and snacks; company parties; and the like should be routine and balanced with recent performance. Interims will often look at these expenses without bias, ensuring they fit within traditional norms.

For each of these areas, it should always be remembered that simplicity is an oft overlooked enabler of overall efficiency.

As Southwest Airlines has proven, flying only one model of plane, reducing boarding complexity by not issuing seat numbers, and flying the same tried and true routes created a simple and profitable model. The remainder of this chapter examines each of these areas of potential operational efficiency in greater detail, providing insights into how Interims approach optimization of these components.

PROFITS

Great companies deliver an above-average (often industry-leading) return on investment, capital, and resources. Profits are used in each of these calculations to provide a consistent method of analysis. By benchmarking the percentages of each line item against appropriate competitors, the biggest areas of opportunity can be easily identified.

Interims add clarity for their clients in surprising ways, including by asking basic questions that result in revealing answers. Many companies fool themselves into believing that problems are not as serious, or opportunities not as large, as they may seem. Interims strip away the fiction and get to the facts, enabling the company to focus on things that matter and will produce results. Profits are a black-and-white, nonsubjective measure of the overall health of a company. In examining profits and the cost components of that equation, Interims identify major business drivers, looking for misalignment with what they would typically see in a healthy company. These could include:

Revenue per Employee—This metric shows the overall effectiveness of an employee base in serving a given level of revenue. If below average, there may be an opportunity for price increases, a change in customers targeted, or performance issues of the sales team.

Cost of Goods—Cost of goods optimization centers on examining the costs of raw materials/components, shipping to/from manufacturing facility, storage, value-added services, rework, quality assurance (QA), final packaging, and labor to produce a particular item. With all of these moving parts and complexities of a global supply chain, there are many factors to be considered and many opportunities for potential improvement. If profits are low, then innovation among these interrelated processes can produce a dramatic and ongoing ROI.

Profitability by Product/Service Line—Driving profitability requires that all products and services earn their shelf inch, providing not only a meaningful return to the organization but also a return greater than another product or service could generate using those same resources. Improving financial performance sometimes requires small individual tweaks or new approaches to increasing velocity (such as bundling) that have an overall cumulative impact. While pruning stale or underperforming products/services creates the opportunity to refocus customers on core offerings, adding dollars to the bottom line by doing fewer things better.

Debt Burden and Interest Expense as a Percent of Revenue—Overcapitalized companies can spend a lot of money on monthly interest payments and financing fees. Companies with excess capital can further become complacent and lose focus on attaining sustainability as long as funds exist to keep the operation alive. Building more profitable models and supporting processes drives higher profits, thus allowing debt to be retired sooner or on schedule without the need to replace the capital. Interims often introduce new ways of structuring debt and gaining access to capital that are not only lower cost, but also provide better scale, creating a meaningful impact on the bottom line and adding confidence to the company.

Fixed Costs—Fixed costs are, by definition, unvarying based on the volume of business. Disproportionately large fixed costs constitute a burden as well as an opportunity for improvement. Interims examine major fixed costs as they compile other analyses and evaluate overall performance using tools and ratios to understand the costs of volume that are currently being served. Optimizing fixed costs creates powerful returns in two major ways. One is by reducing these expenses to match current or short-term transaction volume. The other is to grow revenue by utilizing untapped capacity in specific areas shown to be underutilized, creating powerful economies of scale by producing more at the same cost.

Seeing a company through an unclouded lens, Interims evaluate fixed costs in an unbiased manner, presenting insights that may not be obvious to the executive team. While savings here tend to be one-time endeavors, the impacts can be large. For example, saving $10,000 a month in rent by consolidating facilities creates a positive bottom line and cash-flow benefit every month. In cases where new revenue strategies are developed to fill untapped capacity, organizations need to ensure that revenue growth is realized (ideally through formal scorecard metrics); otherwise, no gains will be attained.

Labor Costs by Function—Each business has different revenue/cost drivers that can be directly mapped to employee costs. Key Performance Indicators (KPIs) on the cost side include labor dollars per unit when assessing unit economics or labor dollars per new account for sales activities. If overall labor costs are too high, Interims will typically perform a functional breakdown of the organization to understand value created by each function as compared to its costs. This assessment further yields insights on areas where the costs of administrative or other non-value-add functions may be excessive.

Product Mix—Small adjustments in the approach to selling existing products and services can prove to be as powerful as a broader *X-Formation* strategy for many organizations. Viewing the cost of creating, stocking, and marketing each item as "fully loaded," Interims often see trapped revenue potential or cost savings that could emerge from building, packaging, selling, and marketing products differently. Optimization includes minimizing opportunity costs such as lost high margin sales due to out of stock situations or poor sales enablement, and eliminating loss leaders that consume resources without generating a return.

Product Return Rates—Assessing returns and service issues/complaints provide obvious clues to *X-Formation* opportunities as these are the ultimate manifestation of a poor process or inefficiency. Fixing these issues not only creates a return in the form of reduced costs for support, repairs, and the like, but can also boost revenue and sell-through as confidence returns to customers or the marketplace.

These are a few of many examples of how Interims approach the process of assessing profits to identify optimization opportunities within a company to quickly identify expense-side improvements.

PROCESS EFFICIENCY

Continuous improvement is a hallmark of excellent companies, with each new level of performance setting the baseline for another new goal. Interims often introduce total quality initiatives or other challenges to the company to reinvent old ways of doing business. They lead by example, diving deep into the key processes to identify improvement opportunities. The growing use of Lean techniques and Six Sigma to reduce waste in manufacturing is well understood. However, such techniques are often implemented with varying degrees of success due to the complex, global, and interdependent supply chains that many modern companies employ. Interims are not experts in everything, so in situations where specialization is required that neither they nor the executive team possess, they will often find specialists to help attain the expected results.

Nonmanufacturing processes must be assessed as well to ensure bottom-line optimization, with tools like Kaizen and workflow analyses that allow for definition and optimization of administrative processes. Interims are experts at sniffing out wasted steps, rework, and busy work. By observing key processes firsthand, interviewing key employees and stakeholders, and measuring the costs of administrative processes, Interims gain a comprehensive understanding of the situation, allowing them to make firsthand observations, not judgments, as they assess opportunities for improvement.

New technology and competitive pressures require constant challenging of the status quo. In dynamic organizations, processes must undergo nearly constant innovation, with any process that has been unchanged for more than a year being a prime candidate for review, especially if the process is heavily utilized or represents a unique differentiator. Sometimes outside auditors may be necessary not only to ensure regulatory compliance, but also to provide expert review of highly specialized processes. One key to creating a culture fueled by employees who are willing to embrace change as the new norm is to clearly communicate not only opportunity for improvement, but also the urgency to act. For change to be realized, the whole organization must understand that the status quo will no longer be acceptable and that the company must change and grow, or it will be left behind by the competition.

Case Study: $10M Invested for $700K in Revenue

A privately held botanical therapeutics company had developed a food supplement by extracting and stabilizing plant polyphenols to address diarrhea in both humans and animals. This product was available in many different forms and formulated for different uses. It was selling a travel product for humans through Amazon.com and agricultural products for porcine and bovine producers through a wholly owned subsidiary. Further complicating its model were four additional products, each with its own unique sales channel. These were private-label products for a multilevel marketing company, a formulation for sale through airport convenience outlets, an SKU for Whole Foods distribution, and an additive for a life-science company.

The company was also running low on cash. Despite all these products and revenue channels, it was generating less than $700,000 in annual revenue. Potential new investors saw the promise of the company's products and intellectual property, but were wary since the company had spent over $10 million to date. An Interim COO was asked by the board to review the current business strategy and decide on which markets to pursue, develop a business plan for growth and fund-raising, and address the high cost of goods.

After looking at the financial opportunities in the various business opportunities it was clear the botanical therapeutics company was trying to do too much at once. The Interim COO identified a low-cost source for contract manufacturing, allowing the company to reduce cost by 75 percent. He then collaborated with the CFO to develop a focused business plan to raise the final investment round needed to get to profitability. As part of the plan, the company would spin off the agricultural subsidiary as a standalone investment and confine consumer sales to the premium grocery channel only. These changes led to a licensing deal which raised $5 million in needed capital.

The Interim led the company in reevaluating its key strengths and identifying leverage points that would provide higher returns on a simplified model. The go-forward strategy was recast to position the business as a provider of core technology, licensing its intellectual property for private label manufacturing.

As the above case study illustrates, many companies have the capability to perform at much higher levels, given the right focus. Optimization activities seek to attain the highest levels of performance that can reasonably be expected, thus creating a highly efficient business engine.

SYSTEMS

Successful companies know large-scale or core business processes are best defined as a series of smaller interconnected processes. The input to each process requires the output from another. This concept, known as the Input-Process-Output (IPO) model, is a common tool Interim CIOs/CTOs use to assess systems and automation, and identify opportunities to add or refine technology to create better efficiency.

Software and underlying processes are often inseparably intertwined, so Interims typically assess underlying procedures and practices, as well as the technology itself, seeking areas of inefficiency. Automating poor processes almost never leads to better results as inefficiencies and other barriers are rarely eliminated. In fact, poor processes add constraints and complications to any technology utilized, thus hampering the performance of new systems or equipment and reducing anticipated return on investment. Often, Interims will introduce new tools to an organization, like formal process decomposition, as outlined below using an Input/Process/Output breakdown, to identify process inefficiencies or bottlenecks.

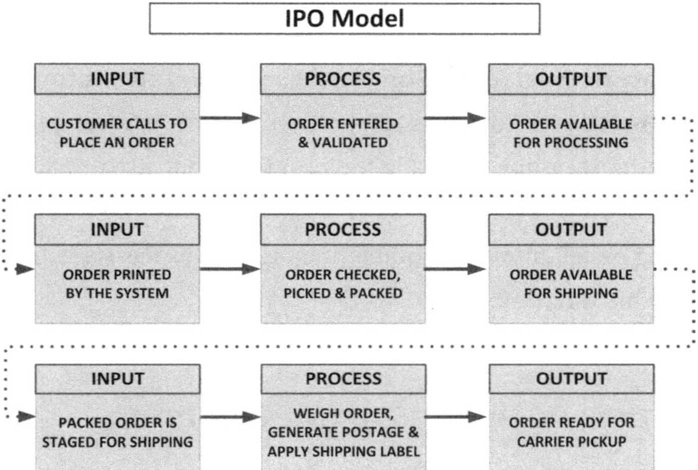

Input-Process-Output Model

While the above example follows the process of a single order, this review can be done on a broader scope. For example, the IPO Model could be used to outline systems needed to go from "Order to Cash" starting with the salesperson pitching a product and following that order through all the systems until the invoice is paid by the customer and the cash is in the bank. This methodical review serves to clarify core processes, identify critical gaps and clearly identify integration opportunities.

It's amazing how many companies struggle to make efficient and effective use of technology to enable business. It is similarly amazing how quickly employees will become accustomed to inefficient processes that require rework or rekeying of data from one system to another. In optimizing performance, Interims tend to zero in on inefficiencies that stem from poor systems integration and the need to create or patch data. Solving these issues once through improved technology or integration not only creates a positive bottom-line impact in the near term, but also provides an ongoing payback on each transaction, in addition to creating better enterprise enablement for any process needing that information.

OPTIMIZING HUMAN CAPITAL (PEOPLE)

Optimizing people is a challenge for companies that struggle to effectively measure the value contributed by each worker. If this information is well understood, the challenge becomes knowing if additional optimization can be accomplished without adversely affecting quality, morale, or related activities. Interims assess the total employee, contractor, and partner costs, including benefits, insurance, and taxes, as compared to tangible results produced, to understand all costs and opportunities.

> **Employees**—In healthy companies, employee optimization is typically improved indirectly by creating more efficient processes that support greater revenue on the same labor costs or through improved organization, a topic discussed in Chapter 8: "Organize." Companies with urgent profitability or cash flow problems may need to consider pay cuts or layoffs to reduce compensation. Optimizing employee costs includes examination of

benefits and other direct employee costs to ensure these expenses are appropriate given the company's size and culture. Interims add particular value to organizations facing tough employee decisions as they have generally participated in more employee *X-Formations* than their executive counterparts.

Contractors—Contractors provide additional specialized horsepower to a company, typically related to projects or areas requiring expertise that does not exist internally. Contractors, by definition, are an on-demand workforce, so throttling their activities up and down to match business cycles and performance creates a powerful and scalable business model, provided the organization approaches contractor labor with this in mind. Optimizing contractor activities starts with analysis of contract costs vs. value by looking at hard metrics related to the work they perform and understanding the costs and benefits of internal and external approaches.

Partners—Similar to contractors, partners need to be measured by the value they create as compared to the cost of the services provided. Interims typically look to measure results and establish shared goals and metrics that ensure a partnership is successful, and often provide fresh thinking in areas that have been put on autopilot. Examples include managing vendor relationships by asking for additional price reductions as volume grows, as well as reimbursement for errors, level of service failures, and the like. Interims tend to also be well versed in creating Requests for Proposals or Quotes (RFPs/RFQs), leading *X-Formation* with key partners and negotiating deals with new vendors.

RAW MATERIALS

It is surprising how few organizations understand the true and complete cost of the products they create. Many companies know the straight cost of raw materials or parts, but become unclear on total transportation, storage, damage and other related costs that should be captured and attributed directly to the product and not to overhead. Interims are skilled in seeing fundamental problems and transformational opportunities in the cost of items. Small reductions in raw material or other component costs can have a dramatic impact on overall margins, especially for high-volume items.

Once these true costs of a product are understood, gross margins at every price tier and volume can be analyzed to ensure models can scale profitably. Healthy margins at the distribution, wholesale, and retail level are critical in driving customer enthusiasm for the product, but oftentimes, these parties or the manufacturer are squeezed as costs rise or the marketplace changes. From a cost perspective, Interims are often the ones to force the organization to assess pet products that do not provide a meaningful return and suck valuable resources away from better-performing and higher-profit items. The next chapter, "Maximize," discusses driving revenue, including pricing models that can be used in addressing low margin items from a sales perspective should these items remain part of go-forward plans.

FIXED EXPENSES AND OVERHEAD

Interims examine fixed costs in ways that are frequently innovative. This includes measuring the return on investment these fixed costs provide as compared to the business each supports. For example, store rent, utilities, common area maintenance, insurance, and the like set the baseline for the minimum performance of a retail location. Warehousing space can be measured by looking at the monthly cost to store each item based on inventory turns and revenue potential, as well as overall storage density and utilization percentage. Office or administrative space must similarly be properly sized to the enablement it provides to the organization and ideally measured in hard dollars. Viewing these costs as a component of overall enablement and performance can lead an organization to dramatically augment its business model. Further, assessing the all-in costs of these internal operations provides a solid baseline for assessing outsourced or third-party opportunities for enablement.

Chapter 8, "Organize," discusses alignment of assets and

people to ensure maximum return on those assets, which can indirectly lower fixed cost ratios through increased output.

DISCRETIONARY EXPENSES

Interim CFOs scrutinize discretionary expenses and focus on correlating benefits to performance and goals. This approach creates awareness of these costs throughout the organization, generating dedication to accomplishing goals as a means to keep, or add, desired benefits or comforts. A positive side effect of engaging the company in this process is increased employee innovation, resulting in programs and policies that create more perceived value for the organization at large, sometimes at lower cost.

PLAN OPERATIONAL CHANGES

With analysis complete, plans are built to transform, innovate, and measure processes at a new level. Interims look first for transformation opportunities that have the highest payback with the lowest effort or risk, and the quickest impact to the company. Sometimes the items that fit these criteria are not the shiny changes the company envisions or those that have the emotional investment from the executive team. Interims confidently provide perception-changing insights based on data combined with experience in similar *X-Formations*, which frequently take the client in an unexpected direction.

> Interims actively identify threats and engage the entire executive team in developing proactive strategies to reduce or remove risk, increasing likelihood of overall success.

The benefit of relatively small but related improvements is often overlooked by organizations yet espoused by Interims. Executive teams trying to improve performance often take a go-big-or-go-home attitude, figuring that major changes need to happen in big, bold strokes. While this is sometimes true, there are often opportunities for smaller innovations that can drive dramatically improved performance, bringing results sooner and reducing overall risk.

Complex, interrelated processes represent ideal candidates for incremental improvement. For these complex processes, true capacity is often poorly understood due to limitations in previous processes which, themselves, restrict overall throughput of the larger process. When the limiting process bottleneck is resolved, the limitation of a downstream process is then felt. One Interim COO illustrates this to clients by asking them to imagine a snake digesting a large meal. The bulge presents a backup due to less throughput at a subsequent step. Once an issue is solved at one step, some downstream process will likely struggle to handle newly increased volumes from preceding steps. Once limitations like this become clear, organizations are able to transform quickly by focusing on a few key pinch points. Interims often help organizations see their specific problem more clearly, allowing for more precise solutions, as well as the ability to anticipate the next likely bottleneck by forward-engineering likely outcomes.

Once the executive team is clear on the plan and in agreement, communicating the plan to the organization along with anticipated impacts is crucial. In this communication, the executive team shows confidence and clarity in addressing opportunities for improvement and provides the basis for employee feedback, ultimately winning the hearts and minds of the staff.

In building plans for transformation, Interims can be more sensitive to risk and active in risk mitigation than their clients. This is born from their practical experience leading large-scale transformation and also the Interim's focus on results and quality execution. By jointly identifying risks, the entire executive team is then able to participate in the process of developing active strategies to reduce or remove risk, increasing the likelihood of overall success.

EXECUTE TRANSFORMATION THROUGH OPTIMIZATION

Interims thrive in leading execution. Using the plans created and the goals established, the executive team is able to move forward with the *X-Formation*. Clients accustomed to the shoot-ready-aim approach of operating (where they start executing before a complete plan with clear goals is in place) are often surprised at how smoothly properly managed execution can be. Interims balance the need for speed with that for quality thinking and demonstrate the benefits of a methodical approach by bringing facts and data forward to drive transformation prioritization and plans.

Once execution begins, Interims often bring new and healthy ways of addressing inevitable issues/surprises and driving execution through to completion. Well-planned *X-Formations* minimize drama, uncertainty, and spotty results that many have come to expect when putting plans for large-scale change into action. Once phase-one changes are implemented, the process begins anew by analyzing new performance levels as a baseline and by looking for incremental improvement opportunities.

SUMMARY

Once strategy has been set, Interims typically look at cost drivers and bottom-line performance to understand where optimization can benefit the company. Optimization, the second *X-Formation* discipline, strives to create improved efficiency, support higher results at the lowest cost, and provide ongoing returns as volume increases.

Optimization efforts are measured by looking at business

processes as well as overall bottom-line results. The ultimate goal is to create an efficient engine that can power increased transaction volume smoothly and profitably. By drilling down into and segmenting detailed cost components, Interims are often able to shed fresh light on where specifically an organization should focus its efforts to gain higher efficiency or effectiveness. Optimization sets the stage for maximization by streamlining supporting processes and creating the ability to serve more demand efficiently, without sacrificing profits or quality.

CHAPTER 7

MAXIMIZE

TOP-LINE INNOVATION

Growing top-line revenue is perhaps the most important benefit that Interims can provide. As the well-known adage states, "Growth solves many ills." Growing companies create more buzz, have an easier time attracting capital and talent, and overall have more opportunities than those in decline or with stalled growth.

The two primary sources of top-line growth are sales to new customers and retention of, and additional sales to, existing customers. Customer health can never be taken for granted and can typically be improved or maximized with fresh sales approaches driven by hard data. These concepts are foremost in the minds of many Interim CSOs/CMOs, as they know it is very difficult to generate sustained sales growth when new sales are offset by significant customer defections.

> The ultimate goal of maximization efforts is to optimally sell ideally priced high-margin products/services to an enthusiastic customer base in properly defined and highly aligned channels.

The *X-Formation* discipline of maximization focuses on growth of the top line. Yin to the yang of optimization efforts, maximization focuses on growing sales dollars, units, gross margins, and customers. The ultimate goal of maximization efforts is to optimally sell ideally priced, high-margin products/services to an enthusiastic customer base in properly defined and highly aligned channels. Maximization focuses effort on innovating value chain processes, which include all activities from presales to postsale customer service that directly impact the customer.

Interims build a great deal of unique knowledge by working with many different clients and learning, in detail, various strategies for identifying and unlocking revenue potential. Clients benefit by learning different approaches based on firsthand experience that would take most executives more than a lifetime to accumulate and guidance working through different items that must be considered in using each approach. Using this knowledge, Interims bring innovative ideas, tools, and proven approaches to selling, marketing, branding, and positioning products and services, using holistic approaches that favor leveraging sunk costs, past investments, and customer goodwill to drive the highest margins with regard to add-on sales.

Interims start by examining sales plans, trends, performance of products and product lines, analyzing production and distribution models, and assessing alignment with the company's sales channels and sales capabilities. Interim CMOs guide companies through the latest disciplines and trends in marketing relevant to each client's situation. This is accomplished by first assessing a company's reach, exposure, brand image, and overall marketing prowess. As with optimization activities, realizing the full value of maximization efforts requires examination of often complex and interrelated value chain processes that cross several, if not all, parts of the organization. Once opportunities and challenges are understood, plans are built to spur innovation of sales and marketing tools and techniques, transforming the organization to drive higher performance. This chapter outlines how Interims assess, plan, and execute transformational sales and marketing initiatives to lead their clients to higher ground.

ASSESS TOP-LINE PERFORMANCE

In assessing the health of sales, marketing, and other revenue-generating parts of a company, Interims first need to be aware of the operational strength and capacity of a company (outlined in Chapter 6: "Optimize"). The operational capacity of an organization has to meet or exceed its demand generation capabilities; otherwise, issues, errors, and costs will increase along with volume. Understanding any anticipated limitations is critical to assessing maximization opportunities. Many retail companies, for example, experience functional breakdowns during peak holiday sales days, like Black Friday and Cyber Monday, when their core processes simply fail once volume exceeds the capacity of people, processes, and systems. While not ideal, extreme situations that tax capacity for short durations are often not the most pressing needs for companies.

Once operational capacity and reasonable volume limits are known, the gap between that volume (allowing for seasonality and peaks) and the current sales volume represents the ideal revenue expansion opportunity. Maximizing revenues within current operational limits also creates a larger bottom-line impact, as the infrastructure supporting higher volume is already in place and being paid for at any transaction volume. Thus, higher real margins are produced on the last transactions through the pipeline in a given business cycle.

Fueled by a solid strategy, optimized core processes and an understanding of optimal transaction limits, an Interim CSO/CRO, CMO, or CEO will typically look at all segments of the value chain for Maximization opportunities:

> **Marketplace**—Assessing the overall state of markets and demand for products or services within each market is the first step in understanding the health of a revenue stream. Assessing the gap between current and desired market position allows organizations to clearly identify

issues that stand in the way of ideal positioning and opportunities that exist to exploit whitespace in the marketplace or areas where competition is weak.

Product Alignment—The best and most powerful product organizations align each product or service in their lineup to create unique value and span the customer life cycle using good, better, and best approaches. The most popular products are further aligned with vibrant marketplaces full of target customers who are highly aligned with the product's value proposition. Interims look for disconnects in these areas to identify opportunities for improved alignment of products to one another or in major sales channels.

Sales and Marketing—Sales and marketing teams and activities ideally are symbiotic. The efforts of these teams (both focused on maximization of business) from lead generation through sale need to be fully aligned to create an efficient and effective value chain. Each message created needs to clearly communicate the unique value of the product(s) and service(s) with messaging tailored to specific target audiences. Channel partners should serve as powerful extensions of the sales organization, driving increased volume with healthy gross margins by showcasing complementary, not competing, items. Weakness or misalignment of sales and marketing activities, or poor performance from an unenthusiastic vendor or partner base, limits performance, providing opportunities for new approaches designed to maximize sales.

Customer Satisfaction and Retention—A churning customer base consumes resources and profits, while a satisfied, energized and expanding customer base drives exponential results with seemingly little effort. Poor customer health, or high churn, is symptomatic of many possible ills, including poorly defined or priced products/services, substandard sales or delivery processes, or misalignment or ineffective positioning within a marketplace. Solving retention issues has both a positive top-line impact by stanching leaking revenue, and also allows for better and more efficient use of value chain resources to drive more business.

MARKETPLACE

A company can face a nearly limitless number of marketplace challenges, including declining demand for its products, significantly increased competition, stale channel expansion strategies, or opportunities lost by not keeping pace with dynamic and volatile markets. Interim CMOs and CSOs/CROs have experience creating sales and marketing excellence using several different techniques to analyze the current market. They lead the company to create action plans designed to maximize sales and amplify the effectiveness of business development strategies by first assessing the current state of affairs. Some techniques Interims use to assess the marketplace include:

Market Research—Analyzing sales performance and opportunities with fresh eyes, Interims often introduce new ways of assessing sales performance and identifying opportunities within target markets. Interims are more likely to approach needs in more holistic ways, looking for as much hard data as possible to substantiate proposed changes. Through market research, analysis of unbiased data on the size of markets, and identifying the needs of potential customers within that market, clear and indisputable findings emerge regarding a company's products and services. Any major misalignments discovered during market research will be included in the overall *X-Formation* plan, as success will be difficult if target markets are not aligned with items being sold.

Competitive Analysis—Hard data showing how products and services stack up against those of major competitors provides several benefits to an organization. The first is clarity on white space within a given market, meaning customer needs that are unmet or underserved. The second is knowledge of strengths and weaknesses of competitors and their specific offerings that is ideally focused on tangible aspects like price, features, guarantees/warranties, bulk discounts, and the like. The third is insight related to pricing within a marketplace and the relative uniqueness of one company's perceived value versus competing products. The result of competitive analysis should be a clear mapping of the company's products and services to each marketplace, identifying the largest opportunities. Models like Michael Porter's Five Forces are useful tools in approaching competitive analysis in a structured manner.[12]

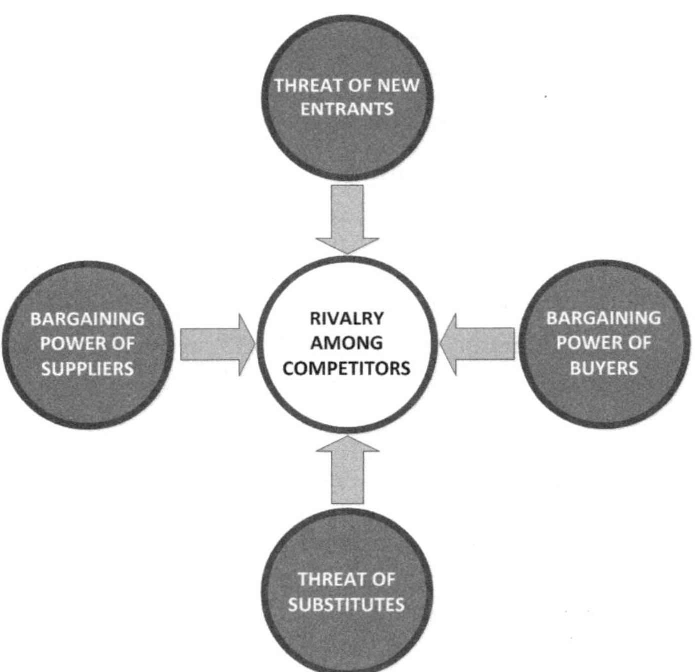

Michael Porter's Five Competitive Forces

12 Michael Porter, "The Five Competitive Forces That Shape Strategy," *Harvard Business Review* (January 2008).

Product / Product Line Performance—Products and services require constant innovation to remain fresh and relevant, especially in fast-moving markets. Further, every product has to earn its spot in the lineup. Many companies produce and support products without understanding the true performance and costs of one item versus another except for overall sales. Others constantly add products without retiring underperforming legacy items, allowing each new product to degrade the performance of legacy items. Interims, with no emotional ties to past strategies, pet projects, or legacy agendas, can provide surprising data-based findings and recommendations to their clients in the area of product line rationalization.

Companies are often shocked to discover that when true costs are examined (those being costs of products, sales and marketing, operations, support, and lost opportunities), some items in the current lineup are losing money. Items that produce low net margins also need to be viewed with a critical eye because these items add unnecessary complexities to operations, consuming valuable resources that could be invested in selling healthier products. By looking at inventory turns by item, sales by category, discount percentages, return rates, and other hard data, Interims paint a vivid picture of products that are working and those that are not.

> Interims, with no emotional ties to past strategies, pet projects, or legacy agendas, can provide surprising data-based findings and recommendations to their clients.

With an understanding of current product and service position within defined markets (and desired markets) and the competitive landscape, organizations can now assess the alignment of sales and marketing resources and processes to efficiently sell into these markets.

PRODUCT ALIGNMENT

Once the highest-performing products are identified, the task at hand becomes finding ways to drive higher volumes of these items, meanwhile deciding what to do with low-margin or other problematic products. Product alignment focuses on factors including:

Product / Product Line Definition—The definition and positioning of products is critical to maximizing sell-through and margins. Data-driven analysis of products clearly shows those that outperform. Sometimes trapped revenue lives simply in the way products and features are defined, and sometimes upselling and cross-selling opportunities are lost in broken lines that fail to meaningfully lead engaged customers to higher-dollar or higher-margin products and services. Product lines should have clearly established benefits that, ideally, support a good-better-best pricing model with powerful hooks into each successive price tier. Throughout this process, Interims challenge their clients to honestly evaluate if all products are earning their position in the portfolio and are delivering not simply appropriate top-line sales, but also bottom-line performance.

Pricing Analysis—Proper pricing drives customer enthusiasm, maintains healthy margins, and provides positive value to the customer as well as the company. In assessing pricing, Interims analyze overall sales volumes, gross margins, and effective discounts by product and by customer to assess the relative health of all products and services. Understanding performance dynamics and the competitive landscape, insight and modeling reveal opportunities for gaining additional revenue on current sales volumes and for selling items in new and profitable ways.

Proper sales and revenue plans can only be built once clarity exists on what an organization sells, to whom and why. When these concepts are clear and backed by a well-defined product strategy, pricing changes can be implemented to unlock trapped revenue. It is surprising that many companies establish the pricing for products or services in a somewhat arbitrary way by simply looking at competing products. The best and most powerful companies peg prices to the value each creates, general market needs, or ideally, specific customer pain points, as these dynamics allow companies and products to transcend from traditionally defined and constrained models into areas where competition is reduced (or nonexistent) and customers are focused on outcomes rather than costs.

Value-Added Services—Value-added services exist in many business models, some as a main line of selling, and some more in the background. Regardless of product or industry, value-added services represent one of the most powerful selling techniques when those services are highly aligned with the needs of customers who are already engaged with a company. Value-added services benefit from being somewhat insulated from price sensitivity, as these transactions piggy-back on the sale of other products/services, and offer the convenience and simplicity of dealing with a single vendor. As a result, these products and services offer the opportunity for additional high margin revenue that is also tightly aligned with services already being delivered or products being consumed. Interims help organizations think about the full potential of a revenue stream, often unlocking powerful add-on revenue. It is shocking how many companies provide valuable services for free that their customers would readily pay for, were they positioned properly.

Bundles and Kits—Similarly, the notion of bundling or kitting several items into a single purchasable unit exists in virtually all sales models. Value meals at quick-service restaurants are so commonplace that shoppers are surprised when there is no such option. A less wide-spread approach is that of productized service offerings. A consulting firm, for example, could charge a flat fee for providing an organizational assessment, developing the associated strategy, and creating the action plan to accomplish, selling these related services as a single item in bundled fashion, increasing perceived value and reducing risk to the buyer. Having worked with companies producing varied products and services across many industries, Interims see firsthand the benefits of powerful bundling and kitting approaches. By bringing these experiences to companies that are reinventing demand models and sales plans, they are able to introduce perception-changing ideas and approaches that result in more powerful and well-rounded sales models.

Bulk Sales—Bulk sales offer the promise of lower per-unit costs to the customer while creating better cash flow, less support per unit as compared to single unit sales, and better overall unit economics for the seller. Bulk sales, however, also offer a strategic advantage to hook customers much more deeply into a company's products or services. Exposing customers to larger quantities of a single item allows not only for higher average order size, but also provides the opportunity for a deeper relationship with a customer as that customer consumes higher volumes of given items. Most people and companies like the notion of getting a deal, and multiunit discounts deliver on this promise while also giving the seller the opportunity to lift prices and margins on single (unbundled) units to drive more adoption of bulk sales offerings.

Recurring Revenue—Recurring revenue is the holy grail of all sales models. It produces the highest multiples when exiting a company and is viewed most favorably by potential sources of capital. Recurring revenue also provides an incredible cash-flow benefit, correlating predictable revenue (often charged at the beginning of a delivery cycle) with the costs associated with delivering that service. Some products and services are oriented to recurring revenue models (e.g. satellite radio). The opportunity exists for many companies to develop new products/services in their core discipline that are maximized for recurring revenue, such as subscription-based transactions, delivery of online content, or sale of annual maintenance plans.

Channel Partners—Channel partners are often overlooked in assessing sales opportunities. Sometimes partners exist but underperform. Sometimes there is no partner strategy. Often, limited one-off partnerships

> are started along the way with unstated expectations and little to no real investment (or results!) from either party. The opportunity for all companies is to define partners that frequently come in contact with target-market customers. Channel partner strategies must always focus on products that add context or value to the partner's business, clearly avoiding any conflicts or products that detract from a partner's core messages. By leveraging a partner's relationship and goodwill with its customers, credibility is easily established, increasing the likelihood of a sale of complimentary products or services. The goal is to create a virtual sales force that can dramatically increase reach and support scale through indirect efforts. The nature of these programs, where the partners earn a commission or other benefit upon sale, pays further dividends by matching the cost of these sales with revenue generated.

Interims are always on the hunt for the biggest and quickest paybacks and prioritize plans accordingly. Understanding the state of products and prices is a critical step in assessing the overall health of sales efforts and opportunities for maximization.

SALES AND MARKETING EFFICIENCY

In assessing sales and marketing functions, Interims look at the internal people, processes, and systems of an organization. With a focus on maximizing sales and marketing efforts from lead generation through customer service, Interims look to measure the results of individual cycles and events, striving for maximum sales dollars per cycle. Basic notions, such as who in the organizations owns a customer, are often hazy within the mind of the leadership team. Failing to understand these concepts threaten the opportunity to attain complete success, as all value-chain processes will be compromised.

When a company finds that its sales and marketing processes are inefficient, ineffective, or both, an Interim CSO or CMO provides fresh approaches to solving stubborn sales challenges. By addressing these challenges previously at many companies, Interims become accustomed to looking for misalignment of sales and marketing efforts, as well as the efficiency of supporting processes. An Interim CSO or CRO looks at hard data spanning the entire customer journey and the major processes within, examining key metrics like total cost per sale, conversion percentage per stage, and cost per lead per source. These veterans of the nonstop demand to fuel ever-increasing sales quotas also look internally to assess sales commission/incentive plans, sales operations, and core processes with an eye to repeatable sales processes that can be measured and utilized to generate ongoing sales.

Interim CMOs or CCOs analyze the overall alignment of products and services with the marketplace messaging.

These individuals analyze brand strength, equity and recognition, and the overall positioning of items in target markets. They assess the alignment of those markets to sales channels and the value of prospects (leads) and qualified leads versus the costs of conversion. By modeling lifetime value (LTV) and understanding fulcrums that can be leveraged to increase loyalty and maximize LTV, Interims often deliver deeper insights than can be gained by simply analyzing cost per conversion.

In all of these activities, the Interim uses proven approaches to lead and teach the organization how to segment its sales activities, pipeline, and customer base, and measure the effectiveness of key activities. This data provides insights into not only the health of the pipeline, but also the potency of the overall sales strategy, tools, and processes, and trapped revenue that can potentially be unlocked. Issues and opportunities discovered in sales and marketing activities serve as the basis for constructing action plans.

CUSTOMER EXPERIENCE AND RETENTION

The final component in assessing maximization opportunities lies in the realm of customer satisfaction. The most potent sales strategies can be undermined by poor customer satisfaction and retention. No matter how effectively companies acquire new customers, if they have significant turnover in their customer base, revenues will suffer accordingly as sales drop out of the bottom of the funnel. To assess customer health and satisfaction, Interims will typically examine several key aspects of the customer experience:

Customer Feedback and Satisfaction Metrics—Interim sales and marketing executives use proven approaches to seek feedback, assess metrics, and define opportunities, including:

Customer Satisfaction Surveys—This tried-and-true approach can provide a solid baseline for overall customer engagement and satisfaction. Updated for the twenty-first century, Net Promoter Score (NPS) is an example of the metric that many companies use as a single overall indicator of satisfaction.

Customer Interaction Forensics—The quantity and nature of all customer communication (good, bad, and informational) can serve as a less overt measure of underlying strength or weakness in serving customer needs and maximizing retention than traditional analysis of complaints. Evaluating help desk or support calls and social media can provide the Interim with a deeper understanding of the strengths and weaknesses of products and services in the eyes of customers, and with a list of common complaints.

Customer Advisory Groups—Advisory groups

comprised of actual customers can provide revolutionary insights into customer pain and pleasure points, especially for companies that manufacture complex products, like software solutions. These interactions allow the seller to gauge overall enthusiasm and hear directly how it can create more value for companies that are already paying them. Turning requests into features can be a great source of low-risk revenue to companies that can operate in this fashion.

Ancillary Operational Data—Transactional data within an organization can yield a wealth of information to Interims who are good at looking for specific pieces of information designed to confirm and quantify suspicions of customer health. By expertly examining return rates, order processing backlog/turnaround time, length of call center calls, length of sales cycle, average ticket size, and customer recency/frequency, Interims help clients develop theories and draw conclusions on the true issues and underlying causes. Further, great clarity regarding areas where the company is most (and least) potent can be gained through a detailed examination of past or current customers by looking at the percentage of sales by customer, examining the gross margin by customer, and breaking down product/service consumption by customer.

Corporate Culture—Some companies are notorious for having a corporate culture that treats the customer as an inconvenience at best, while others such as Zappos, are world renowned for having customer satisfaction embedded deep within their culture and corporate DNA. One veteran Interim cited the example of a technology company that had a culture in which customer needs were treated as an inconvenience. At this company, a postimplementation debriefing meeting was held to gather feedback from a recent project, where the installation team was asked for its view of how the project had gone. Team members universally reported the project had gone well and that the installation was a success. However, when asked how the customer felt, the team universally agreed that the customer was very unhappy, showing clearly that the culture of this company was focused on internal achievement rather than customer satisfaction.

Customer Points of Contact—An Interim CSO/CRO will typically work to identify the experience of the customer through all points of contact and at all levels of the organization. By taking a holistic approach to understanding the overall value chain, then segmenting that approach to each service or support activity, inconsistencies in the service provided at each point in the customer life cycle are identified. These findings help frame the overall importance of activities that may previously have been considered siloed or unimportant in the grand scheme of things. As the saying goes, a process is only as strong as its weakest link.

By way of example, one software company had a very stable product that was popular with the users. Customer support at the user level was consistently rated as outstanding. Nevertheless, this company was in serious danger of significant customer losses amid dwindling product enthusiasm. While maintaining excellent contact at the user level, the company completely failed to maintain any relationships at the decision-maker level. Since the market was undergoing rapid change, decision-makers made the assumption that the current vendor was not keeping pace and were actively seeking alternatives they considered to be more state of the art. The vendor was not involved at all in helping to influence the strategic direction of the customer. By only measuring and maximizing sales to new accounts, this company lost sight of the importance of ongoing business development, support, and critical touch points with the customers that were already paying it money!

Interims assess the mechanisms through which clients can engage customers, helping to define the purpose and desired experience for each customer profile. Social media and more deconstructed forms of customer interaction have now become commonplace, complicating the ability to deliver the right information at the right time based on the customer's need. Part of the value proposition for many organizations engaging seasoned Interim CSOs and CMOs is realized in bringing stale or even antiquated methods of fostering customer engagement into the present by helping clients build out strategy and plans that include use of modern communication methods, as well as create world-class supporting processes for using new and unfamiliar means of engagement and response.

Company Accessibility—One of the most frustrating customer challenges is having a problem and not knowing who to contact for help, or having a contact but not receiving a timely response. Interims quickly evaluate if this is an issue. In one example, a well-known software vendor changed its support system to save money. The new technical support system delivered a recorded message that it no longer took phone calls and only worked through online chat. While issues could be resolved, the fact that customers could no longer talk to anyone directly created a significant negative reflection on the company.

The levels of service offered, cost of those services, and quality of those services as compared to the marketplace all represent opportunities for maximizing revenue. Assessing these opportunities early enables an Interim to build plans for proper customer engagement that are in line with overall maximization goals and plans.

Interims can be particularly effective at helping companies clearly see the benefits of improved customer satisfaction across many spectrums, resulting in improved financial performance, increased sales, and reduced expenses.

Case Study: Rebuilding the Revenue Model

No industry is more affected by rapid disruptive change than those in software development. During the 1990s, a large and well-established enterprise software company was experiencing years of declining revenue and persistent losses. The business was part of a larger conglomerate that did not have a core competency in creating software solutions. The management team had been in place for some time and was generally capable but had lost its grasp on innovation. There was little oversight from the parent company, and the continuing losses, while significant, were easily absorbed by the much larger entity, allowing malaise to take root. A change in the leadership of the conglomerate prompted a review of all businesses in the portfolio, highlighting issues at the software company.

The parent company decided to bring in an Interim CEO to quickly evaluate strategic options for the business. After a brief period, the Interim CEO determined:

1. The Management Team's focus was on effective internal operations. This focus carried through to customer support activities, resulting in high customer satisfaction at the user level.
2. The software platform was based on old technology but was very stable. There were many new entrants to the market offering leading-edge solutions using modern technology. The management team relied almost exclusively on industry reports for their view of the market, conducting virtually no first-hand discussions with decision-makers at existing or prospective customers. As a result, significant investments were being made in the development of new products for which there was little demand and had virtually no prospect of success. Key customers were making decisions to move to competitors based on a perceived lack of innovation due to poor communication.

The Interim CEO assembled a cross-functional team of key company leaders. Using several innovative techniques, including scenario planning, the team developed very innovative and inexpensive solutions that could move the technology to the current era. The team further developed a series of ancillary services that could augment revenue from the existing customer base.

Following this, the Interim CEO and key senior executives visited the decision-makers' at major customers to communicate their plans for improving the solution. With a renewed product strategy, reenergized customers and new marketable features in the solution, revenue began to grow and the company returned to significant profitability. This company, like so many others, had good bones but had lost its way. The Interim, assessing the business without ties to past decisions and with deep experience in maximization, was able to use proven approaches to help this great company surmount these challenges and regain health.

PLAN VALUE-CHAIN IMPROVEMENTS

As insights emerge during the assessment phase, opportunities become clear, and plans start to develop. Typical findings range from quick hits, which are designed to create immediate wins and to bring value forward, to long-term *X-Formations* that inherently require more planning with varying levels of cost, complexity, and payback. In planning the ensuing changes, Interims look for the highest return on the lowest investment, with investments being the time, people, money, and assets required for the transformation. Minimally Viable Products (MVPs) are often defined and planned as these represent a quick manifestation of value, producing benefit more quickly than if the full solution were developed all at once. Developing an MVP further increases focus on those features deemed to be most beneficial, by minimizing the scope of activities.

Maximization efforts often occur in addition to other organizational changes, such as those outlined in the other chapters of Section 2. Therefore, quality planning of major changes must be aligned with other major initiatives to minimize risk and unintended consequences. Interims actively look for related items, or dependencies, to understand efficiencies that could be gained by bundling related changes together and executing them at the same time.

Planning also includes consideration of communication plans, with many maximization efforts having both internal and external, or customer-facing, plans. Internal plans are designed to prepare the organization for change, clearly communicating impacts to sales, customer service, or other core processes, as well as any policy changes such as compensation/commission plans and pricing or warranty changes. External communication plans position products and services for sale, targeting messages around marketplace dynamics and brand development and positioning, as well as enabling channel partners and resellers.

Once complete, the plan is shared with the organization at large, or at least those directly impacted in the case of smaller changes. At this point, the team moves on to execution, but it should be known that in most cases, execution of parts of the plan has already begun.

Some problems are easier to solve than others, and some opportunities cannot wait until a complete plan is developed. A typical interim engagement begins with, or is created by, an important need within a company. Whether the need is related to capitalizing on a large opportunity or fixing persistent problems, there are typically course corrections that can begin soon after an Interim starts working with a client. Typical strategies are to quickly assess the overall company or department for major fires, define immediate needs, plan near-term actions, and execute on that plan while taking a larger view and building a longer-term plan.

EXECUTE VALUE-CHAIN INNOVATION

With a clear plan in place, focus turns to executing on short and longer-term plans, each segmented by phase and with clearly stated goals. Often maximizing sales and revenues amounts to several small initiatives that need to be accomplished. Other times, major transformation of the company, culture, or overall approach to market needs to be undertaken, creating a driving theme for the initiative. These could include transitioning to a customer-centric culture, entering new markets or leaving existing ones, repositioning products and pricing, moving to/from direct sales and partnership models, and the like.

While executing the plans, measuring progress in an unbiased manner is critical to ensuring that results are meeting or beating expectations. If not, course corrections need to be defined using a similar assess-plan-execute approach. Measuring progress typically takes the form of a scorecard, dashboard, Key Performance Indicators (KPIs), or the like. For maximization efforts, it is critically important that data related to opportunities, leads, or the sales funnel are objective in nature. A weekly weighted sales pipeline value, for example, is of little use if the deals within the pipeline are inaccurate with respect to the true status, deal size, or other factors.

Interims are effective at helping companies implement and execute these types of changes with confidence due to their experience in leading large-scale *X-Formations*. While most plans do not succeed exactly as written, Interims expect challenges as they calmly lead the organization, making necessary course corrections as results are seen and issues encountered. Many Interims are great teachers, taking time to mentor those around them regarding new approaches to problem-solving.

SUMMARY

Maximization is the execution discipline of generating more top-line revenue. Interims take a complete view of maximization opportunities by first assessing the effectiveness of current products and services, then identifying opportunities for new sales channels, marketing strategies, products, bundles, add-on options, and partners.

Once defined, Interims lead the organization through building plans for transformation by looking for areas of highest payback and lowest cost or effort, those that will deliver measurable results as quickly as possible. They confidently lead the organization in executing the plans developed, measuring results, and reexamining the plan when results fall short.

CHAPTER 8

ORGANIZE

MAXIMUM ALIGNMENT = MAXIMUM RESULTS

Effective companies are organized in many ways to achieve great results. Al Ries, marketing expert and author, illustrates the power of focus using light energy as an analogy. The sun, emitting billions of kilowatts of energy, will only give us here on earth sunburn. A laser uses a tiny fraction of that amount of energy yet can cut steel.[13] A key to optimizing an organization is ensuring complete alignment from top to bottom, creating laser-like focus on that which matters most. Corporate organizatión includes not only the way a company's functions, leaders, and employees are structured, but also the alignment of products, assets, and strategies to successfully accomplish the organization's mission.

---

13 Al Ries, *Focus: The Future of Your Company Depends on It* (New York: HarperCollins, 2005).

This section has so far outlined the execution disciplines of: strategizing, optimizing, and maximizing, with optimization and maximization efforts producing the biggest results when built upon great strategy. As this diagram illustrates, the final *X-Formation* discipline, that of organizing, wraps strategy, maximization, and optimization activities, increasing or decreasing the effectiveness of all pieces.

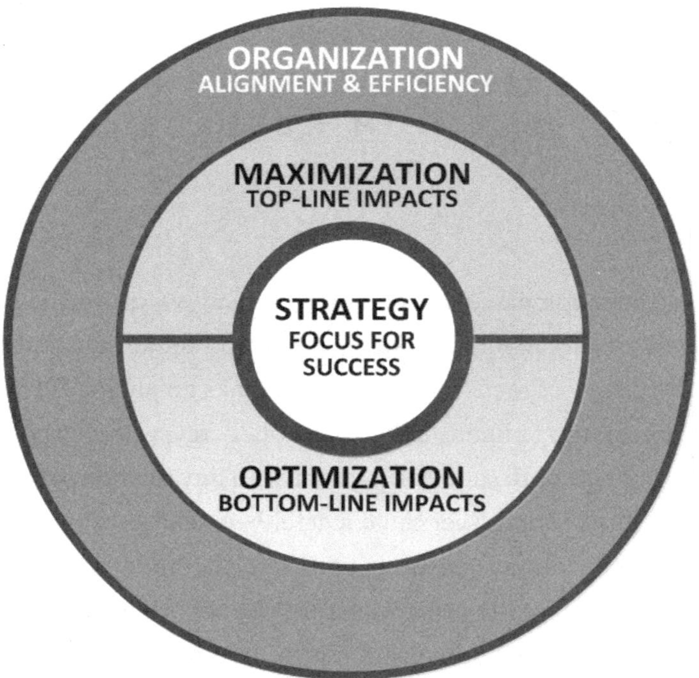

Ineffective or loosely organized companies struggle to achieve results, while highly aligned organizations gain consistent results, sometimes through brute-force methods built on lesser or weaker strategy and plans.

Great companies utilize their organization as a competitive advantage, producing consistent and superior results by harnessing the power of alignment to minimize distractions and inefficiency. Interims view people, products/services, physical plant, technology/systems, equipment, and other assets as investments that must yield a meaningful ROI. These assets are often looked at in the context of individual performance rather than total enterprise enablement. The proper alignment of major assets makes all efforts easier, creating higher results on similar or reduced effort, thus supporting increasingly efficient operations and continually increasing sales. Other positive benefits of great organization include improved employee morale through clarity of role, measurement of results, and improved communication. Thus, achieving optimal organization and alignment of these assets is critical to realizing the full value of these investments.

> Interims help the Leadership Team establish additional skills, knowledge, and operational frameworks that enable the company to gain traction through alignment of critical assets.

Interims often enter situations where there is some degree of organizational dysfunction. As a result, they are experienced at understanding organizational dynamics, separating solid performers from excuse makers, assessing the company's structure, and ultimately building an organization that can execute on the company's vision.

In this chapter, we discuss how Interims assess, plan, and execute on opportunities to gain total organizational alignment designed to deliver lasting results.

ASSESS ASSET ALIGNMENT

With a solid strategy defined and clear plans underway to optimize bottom-line effectiveness and maximize top-line revenue, the main barrier to attaining ultimate success typically results from issues of alignment. Alignment strives to clearly define the organization's structure and create efficient deployment of all major assets, providing a framework for continued excellence and innovation. In assessing organizational effectiveness, Interims may look at the following main areas:

People—People represent the largest investment for most companies. Bringing the right people into a company, clearly defining each role, measuring each person's value, aligning everyone to create accountability and providing them with a clear vision for the future are all critical to maximizing employee performance and enabling success. Interims are great at minimizing emotions and drama as they engage the organization in assessing its people components. They do this by sharing similar challenges they faced at other companies, best practices, objective measures (data), and other experiences to remove doubt by focusing on positive outcomes of any anticipated changes.

Processes—Well-organized processes are repeatedly used by an organization to create value for customers, partners, and internal groups. Many companies fail to view the effort, cost, and tradeoffs required to create excellent processes as either valuable investments or important barriers to competition. Great processes are those that are tightly focused on achieving the company's mission, spanning both the value and supply chain to produce ongoing and ever-increasing returns.

Interim COOs are often engaged by companies to create next-generation operational strategies and approaches, only to find that the existing processes can produce dramatically better results through incremental improvements and a focus on proper alignment between major enabling processes throughout the organization. In assessing process alignment, efficiency and effectiveness must both be considered to ensure that not only are maximum cycles and throughput obtained, but also proper quality and results from those cycles.

Technology/Systems—Information systems and enabling technologies often represent not only an investment in physical assets (computers, software, technology workers, etc.), but also in many related hard, soft, and carrying costs. Ongoing need for developers, apps or plug-ins, hosting, and other ongoing recurring costs, as well as sudden and often urgent support costs, like those required to combat malware, hackers, or integration problems, can greatly deteriorate the performance of these assets. Dysfunctional or severely constrained systems limit opportunities for enterprise-wide alignment and limit possible results. The impact of great information systems and automated processes is often game changing, increasing the importance of assessing and planning these items across the organization.

Interim CIOs and CTOs assess information systems within the context of the value chain each creates, as well as the level of integration each downstream system requires. Stove-piped solutions constrain value and results by segregating data, limiting its usefulness to only a specific department or group of users, and often requiring significant additional effort to rekey critical information into other systems. The best information systems are designed to utilize an enterprise data model that allows a piece of information to be created once and used forever, serving every need.

Equipment—As with information systems, each piece of manufacturing equipment typically participates as one step in a series of interrelated processes. Equipment must fully enable optimized performance of the step(s) for which it is responsible and also integrate properly with equipment that gives input and receives output. The value of one piece of equipment can be meaningfully reduced by bottlenecks created by equipment with suboptimal throughput earlier in the process.

Interim Chief Manufacturing Officers (CMOs) or Chief Production Officers (CPOs) assess the organization of equipment and related production technologies in light of current volume versus maximum capacity, lead/load times, dry/curing/wait times and other steps that represent the full process chain. Often this examination identifies additional opportunities to use existing equipment in new and innovative ways by focusing on gaining fuller utilization of equipment and leasing excess capacity to others.

Enabling Assets—These assets are utilized for special types of problem-solving or enablement that are not captured specifically above. These assets are often specialized to a specific job function (3D printer or high-end graphics tablet), facilitate transition between major process steps (forklift, or delivery truck), or offset and reduce another cost (cardboard bailer that allows waste to be bundled and sold to remanufacturing companies). Enabling assets can also include items such as a physical plant, specialized tools, and safety equipment, depending on the company and its approach to utilizing assets such as these. In general, any major investment that is customized to a company's specific needs is an enabling asset.

> While perhaps not traditionally viewed as an asset that needs alignment, a building, or a physical plant, it needs to yield a return based on the type and volume of products or services it supports. High-growth physical product companies (manufacturers/distributors/retailers), for example, know firsthand that a properly sized and configured physical plant can greatly enable transaction flow, while an undersized or poorly configured building will dramatically impact throughput, quality, and safety. Missing, improper, poorly maintained, and poorly sized enabling assets all represent opportunities to unlock trapped capacity and recapture costs from inefficiency.

The remainder of this chapter will explore these areas in more detail in the context of assessing overall organization of major assets, then planning and executing changes designed to improve overall alignment across the enterprise.

PEOPLE

One of the most difficult challenges for fast-moving companies can be honestly assessing employees' performance and appropriately identifying trapped potential living in either workers with more capacity or those whose natural abilities that could best be used in another position. Seasoned Interims are experts at seeing opportunities to unlock the full potential within existing employee ranks, as well as those inevitable anchors that drag a company down through poor performance, misalignment with the company's culture or values, or both. Nowhere is this more present than in the manner in which people are organized within a company.

People alignment in an organization essentially boils down to having the right people in the right seats doing the right tasks. This notion has been espoused by many business performance gurus, including Jim Collins (*Good to Great*), Gino Wickman (*Traction: Get a Grip on Your Business*), and Verne Harnish (*Scaling Up*).

> **Right Positions**—Often referred to as defining the right seats, this best practice is devoted to functionally decomposing a company into not only its core departments, but also the positions within that department and, most importantly, the key accountabilities for any person who holds that position.
>
> While all companies have common functions such as sales and marketing, operations and finance/administration, each company looks somewhat different, tailoring functions and role definitions to its particular needs. Areas of poor overall performance always provide a great reason to assess if roles are properly defined and if each function is reporting up to the right place in the organization. The roles, functions provided, and people assigned are all placed into an accountability chart, creating clarity as to who does what in the organization. Interestingly,

many companies simply create organizational (org) charts listing names and titles, often with no reference whatsoever as to what each person is supposed to do. While there are other ways to establish and communicate who does what in an organization, one veteran CEO noted that in his experience, "companies that use only an org chart often suffer from lack of clarity in regard to roles defined and problems with accountability."

As workplaces become deconstructed in many ways (open-air offices, reliance on contractors or other third parties, and an ever-increasing remote workforce), the accountability chart is often blurred, with many companies failing to achieve clarity of role and purpose across the enterprise. The accountability chart creates absolute clarity on these matters. It provides the added benefit of creating a baseline for reviewing employee performance, and it serves as the basis for job postings, interview and review documents for each function.

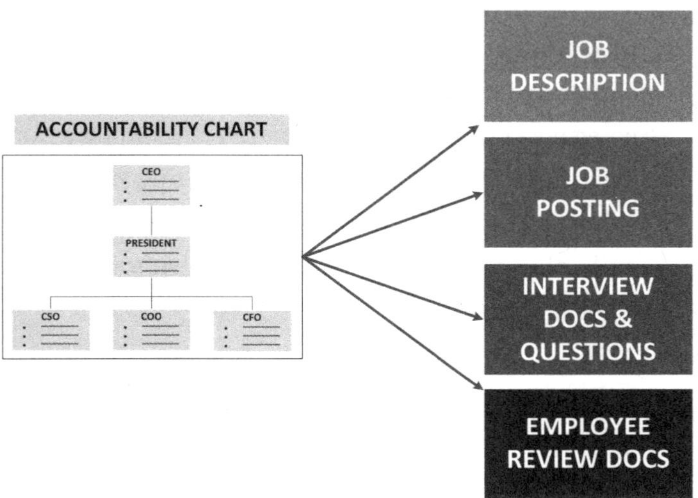

Accountability Chart: The Basis for Employee Documents and Standards

Accountability charts work for most organizations regardless of how flat or vertical they are. The exception is organizations employing a matrixed structure. In a matrixed organization there is no direct reporting structure as the organization focuses on horizontals and verticals, with the intersection representing a function or job. For example, an employee with software development skills and customer service skills in answering technical questions would report to two different bosses, depending on which role that person was filling at a given time (developing new software or providing technical support). This scenario often leads to allocation and prioritization conflicts. Matrixed organizations can benefit from proper role definition and accountability by clearly defining the expectations of each role that person might fill, along with identifying the manager for that area. Once accomplished, each employee needs to be conscious of which role he or she is filling at any given time and success criteria while sitting in that seat. However, conflict over resources and priorities are less easily solved, explaining why most Interims favor hierarchical structures.

It should further be noted that many companies are using Agile/Kanban approaches for software development or other functions, which typically do not fit well into a pure hierarchical structure. Agile principles are built around self-managing teams that typically operate in two-week sprints. These teams work cooperatively with little formalized direction. Agile organizations can use an accountability chart by defining non-Agile roles in a traditional/hierarchical fashion using pools of resources that are allocated to specific Agile teams for each sprint.

Right People—This principle refers to having the right people filling the positions described in the accountability chart. The right people for a company are assessed based on the skills a person possesses and the cultural match of individuals to the company in general. There are many great resources for finding high-performing people with skills matched to a company's needs, for example *Topgrading* by Brad Smart. In the book *Traction: Get a Grip on Your Business*, Gino Wickman further adds the belief that everyone in a company must "Get" and "Want" their role, skills that are separate from the "Capacity" to do the job.[14] Wickman calls this GWC, insisting that ideal employees must Get the role (fundamentally understand how the job is done and how success is achieved), Want the role (not the same as wanting to collect a paycheck for doing the job), and have the Capacity to do the job well (skills to perform the job and time/bandwidth to perform job-related functions well). Surprisingly, these finer points escape many organizations and leaders as they consider the ideal staff for given roles.

The right people for a company also need to be a good cultural fit. Core values represent the soul of a company and employees who fail to share these beliefs often erode enthusiasm and morale. Through alignment on mission and principles, great companies create an impassioned workforce that is fully bought into a company's purpose and ways of working. The best companies openly communicate and put to use core values, rewarding individuals who exhibit these values through tangible actions.

Regardless of how individuals ultimately come to occupy their positions, a best practice is to measure every person's performance using hard data that is tightly correlated to key success factors for that role. A call

14 Gino Wickman, *Traction: Get a Grip on Your Business* (Dallas: BenBella Books, 2011), 99–102.

center employee, for example, might be measured on calls per hour, overall call satisfaction rating, or ideally, both. By creating clear role definitions and measuring performance with data that is directly related to the performance of each person performing that function, it is easy to see how well each employee is performing relative to overall goals and as compared to their peers.

The best people in well-defined positions can still suffer from organizational issues. Some recurring offenders often cited by Interims include:

Unclear Vision—The pace of business and ever-increasing variables that need to be considered and monitored often allow people to see the trees but not the forest. A clear vision that is shared by everyone in an organization is critical to helping each person understand the unique added value their role creates for the company. This understanding creates clarity, fueling enthusiasm and team spirit, as well as alignment. Many times, the exercise of trying to establish a crisp and clear vision teaches a company that it is not as certain or focused in the mission as it believed, thus creating a large and basic issue sure to hamper performance until resolved.

Unclear Decision-making Process—A significant source of dysfunction in organizations is an unclear decision-making process. Decision-making by committee, relitigating each decision multiple times, or constantly deferring decisions to upper management are all symptoms of a broken process and likely poor accountability. Decision-making authority needs to be clear and delegated to the people in the organization closest to the action, allowing the company to benefit from the efforts of many while also creating opportunities for many to participate in a more meaningful way by stepping up.

Problematic Reporting Structure—The accountability chart clearly shows how each function in an organization reports up to the top. Sometimes, and often with people who fill multiple roles within a company, functions report up to areas of the company that do not make sense. For example, one Interim COO recently helped resolve an issue with long order backlogs at a distribution company. The company had order processing reporting up to sales as order fulfillment was considered part of the value chain while inventory control reported up to operations as a supply chain function. The two teams had conflicting priorities and methods of doing their work, creating delays, inefficiency, and finger-pointing. Once both functions reported up to the COO, issues became clearer, problems were resolved cooperatively, and sales benefitted by higher customer satisfaction due to faster turnaround time.

More than One Name in a Box—As the saying goes,

"If more than one person is accountable, then no one is accountable." Not only is having more than one name in a given role a problem for accountability, but it also points to opportunities for simplification. While it is fine to have multiple people performing the same exact function (each is accountable for 100 percent of the role as defined when performing those duties), it is problematic to have two or more people sharing a role where together they are accountable for the result as a duo. Accountability should not be confused with the action of doing a task. Rather, individuals accountable for something own the result along with its timeliness and quality. Many managers and executives are accountable for results produced by the efforts of their teams or even outsourced partners.

When a company is not properly organized, an Interim may be the first person to realize the symptoms of the underlying causes listed above. These symptoms include:

Poor Plans or Direction—When parts of an organization are struggling with no clear plan for improvement, this typically points to either a failure of leadership or poor alignment with the company in general. Leadership failures are clearly shown by looking at the functional definition for that role to assess if performance is in line with expectations. Alignment issues stem from a lack of the ability to coordinate the individual pieces of major business drivers across different functions properly. This results in directing resources in an ineffective manner that is misaligned with the company's mission, or from sending mixed messages that muddle priorities or have nonspecific goals.

Poor Culture and Malaise—Culture thrives when companies share a common vision and hire people who approach work in similar ways and share a set of basic values. Many companies believe culture forms as a result of actions or events the company performs to breed enthusiasm and camaraderie. In reality, orchestrated efforts designed exclusively to grow a culture when one does not exist are artificial and rarely produce any meaningful or lasting results. Rather, by creating a workforce of compatible personalities who share a similar (but not homogeneous) belief system, culture emerges as a natural byproduct for the enthusiasm they share and cooperation they exhibit in performing their jobs.

Drama—Lack of clarity is a breeding ground for drama, infighting, end runs and other forms of bad behavior. As temporary dwellers in organizations, Interims are able to spot these types of disruptions as being signs of other issues. In being measured by the results they produce, Interims are also keen on having focused and happy teams around them. Energy that is wasted on disruptive behaviors cannot be applied to *X-Formation* efforts and diminish the value an Interim, or any executive, can deliver. As drama and complete results are at direct odds, Interims tend to be the ones who identify and address these behaviors early on to ensure that positive and healthy relationships can take root and aid in the attainment of the company's overall mission.

Buck Passing—Interims are transparent and accountable for their results, good or bad. Employees or executives who blame others while excusing their own behavior are masking some sort of issue. Interims are skilled at discovering such issues, reminding everyone that results are what matters and that each person in the organization needs to be accountable for his or her actions and results. In fact, it is often Interims who bring new and healthy practices to a company by letting everyone know that mistakes are acceptable, provided lessons are learned and a commitment is made to never repeat a mistake. Honest and healthy discussion of issues is one of the most important skills an organization can form, as issues that go unaddressed for long periods of time have a way of impacting a company full force at the least opportune times, or so it seems.

For example, we know of one Interim who goes to such great lengths to establish complete transparency and accountability to his clients that he details all accomplishments and activities on every invoice he submits.

While not expected or required, this Interim does this, he says, "because it forces me to be mindful of creating tangible value/results every billing cycle. When it becomes hard to find items to list, then I know there is either other trouble brewing that needs to be addressed that is limiting my progress, or it is time for me to move on because we've accomplished most or all of our goals."

Errors—Regardless of cause, errors are a tangible measure of how well a task (or process) is being accomplished. Interims follow the smoke thrown off by errors in an attempt to understand the root causes and the true costs of these all-too-common inhibitors of maximum results. Often, core issues and the symptoms these create are not simply related to one task or step in the process, but rather larger organizational misalignment.

Poor Throughput—Like errors, slower-than-expected throughput of any core process is a symptom of larger challenges, oftentimes the result of poor alignment. Basic concepts like target output/yield, acceptable quality criteria, and ideal labor costs are often not understood by all individuals involved in major processes, but are often different throughout an organization. Manufacturing, for example, may be completely unaware that the product development group is measured on attainment of theoretical cost projections. Regardless of what is misaligned or misunderstood, these types of issues can only be solved by addressing overall alignment of people and assets throughout an organization because a single group does not have the responsibility or ability to control all factors impacting the results.

By working at the top of many different companies, Interims see the impacts of poor organizational structure frequently and firsthand. Many times the organizations that complain loudest about poor accountability are missing the basic tools required to define roles clearly, provide employees with necessary resources to accomplish their jobs effectively, and support all employees with a solid structure where like functions roll up to an ultimate owner. Interims understand the complexity of making changes to the organization of people or departments. Most companies do not have the same depth of experience and the accompanying *X-Formation* management principles required to execute personnel changes confidently with certainty of outcome. An Interim's calm and steady hand on the tiller creates clarity and resolve with other executives on the team, as findings from assessment activities bring transparency to issues and as necessary changes emerge.

PROCESSES

Process alignment is not necessarily the same activity as process optimization. In Chapter 6: "Optimize," we saw how process innovation occurs when looking for efficiencies and savings that can be realized in accomplishing tasks, and executing individual or tightly related processes. Process alignment speaks to the need to harmonize complex enterprise-wide processes that require participation from many different business units.

Processes that span an organization are, by nature, segmented. For example, the major process that starts with a sales lead, converts the lead to a customer, sells the customer a product, delivers a product, supports that product, and accounts for the sale may span five major areas of the company. Process innovation efforts often focus on excellence or efficiency within a given segment of a long process without too much concern for upstream or downstream opportunities. Assessing the organization of major process steps across an enterprise and where accountability exists for major KPIs or other measurable criteria allows Interims to see opportunities for creating better results through alignment. By understanding the capacity of each part of related processes, Interims often identify low hanging fruit that can lead to dramatic improvements in enterprise performance by focusing only on one inefficient part of a larger process.

By examining the totality of results, Interims tend to be the ones to recognize process alignment issues within a company. This type of experience ultimately reduces risk and opens new opportunities for *X-Formation* of underperforming portions of a business and its core processes. This process also identifies processes that may be in conflict, causing different parts of the company to come together with a new understanding that if one part of the process fails, the company itself fails.

SYSTEMS/TECHNOLOGY

Technology and business processes are intertwined in an inseparable way in today's corporate environment. The reality of these dependencies is that a company's automated or technology-based processes are only as strong as the weakest part. Strong processes backed by poor technology become fragile and overly complicated. Incredible technology fails when a company improperly utilizes its capabilities or refuses to embrace new and innovative ways of doing business. Daily Interims work with companies that have come to accept crippling barriers and poor performance as the norm, giving up hope or the chance to be become excellent simply because of self-imposed, or perceived, limitations.

Innovation in enterprise-wide processes is further complicated by the reality that changing one part of the process or system often creates a domino effect of changes and impacts to other systems and parts of the organization. Quality Interims are skilled at multidimensional problem-solving, taking a huge number of variables and alternatives into account as they lead organizations through positive change. In solving problems for bigger or more complex organizations, a typical Interim is able to help a client not only address immediate challenges, but also anticipate complications that are likely to emerge in the future. By helping companies imagine their future, Interims provide solid leadership and decision-making anchored to current needs with an eye to future challenges that should be anticipated.

Interim CIOs and CTOs, for example, have helped countless companies identify limitations of their existing solutions, assess the features/functions required, and avoid common pitfalls of those less experienced. Companies engaging an Interim benefit from countless hours of real-world experiences, allowing that company to gain from perspectives far in advance of those they could expect internally. For example, one accomplished Interim CIO has successfully implemented over 70 million dollars in enterprise technology with many Fortune 1000 companies. He now typically works with companies sporting $5 million to $100 million in annual revenues, with dramatically smaller IT budgets. By having solved enormous challenges on a global scale for very complex organizations, this Interim is able to add insights and strength in execution that many of his clients could not hope to find or afford long-term. He is further able to help these companies understand the best choices with smaller budgets, charting a path forward that often spans several major initiatives, each designed to layer on top of previous solutions spreading the investment over time.

ENABLING ASSETS

Physical plant and related assets exist to support and fuel a business, but many organizations lose sight of this fact shortly after purchase. Aligning physical assets (machinery, buildings, vehicles, and even capital) is essential to achieving peak performance and maximizing the return on some of a company's most important investments.

Metrics like ROI, asset utilization percentage, sales per square foot, and cycles planned vs. realized are just some indicators that correlate to the use of a given asset. By calculating maximum output at a company's current scale, a company can see opportunities to improve performance by scaling to optimum capacity. Major assets have a cost of use that exists regardless of volume. While oversized infrastructure costs can be crushing at low volumes, at higher volumes, these assets enable top performance at low cost. Once organizations understand true break-even and maximum profit points of major assets and the processes each supports, plans can be developed with specific goals to take the most valuable processes to the next level.

PLAN FOR OPTIMAL ALIGNMENT

With assessment of overall organizational alignment complete, plans for transformation can begin. As a process requiring organization of major assets might imply, plans for reorganizing a company's employees, processes, systems, or other supporting assets require more care in planning and execution than those with less at stake.

The most common type of reorganization that companies undertake is that of people. Assessing issues, defining desired changes, and planning and communicating people changes often requires a great deal of time. It is important to do it right the first time and to eliminate the risk of the reorganization going poorly. Interims typically help their clients not only with identifying needs and planning changes, but also counseling the executive team on best practices in approaching these complex issues and creating appropriate internal and external messages.

Areas of the highest payback and lowest cost/complexity/risk typically provide the most obvious opportunities for improvement. One challenge of company reorganization is that scenarios are often all or none, where executing only a portion of the full change either does not make sense (due to other impacts) or will not produce a meaningful result. As multidimensional problem solvers, Interims tend to be skilled at helping their clients forward engineer the full scope of changes to see likely outcomes.

With these factors understood, solid transformation plans are built and communicated to the company at large, taking care to properly message any personnel impacts. Any time people are impacted in a major negative or positive way, it is critically important to ensure that positive messaging is used to create enthusiasm and limit fear. It's funny that many people are fearful and skeptical of any change, even those that seem positive to others. As one Interim Executive says, "With people changes, I measure like ten times and cut once because a botched rollout or poor messaging makes everything else much harder."

Organization-wide changes must be executed in coordinated fashion for all areas of the business involved. Plans are typically created by function, detailing the changes, anticipated benefits, and any known issues or risks that need to be addressed. These plans must also include all financial aspects including the budget for the transformation to ensure that the organization is able to make it through the full execution successfully.

Changes that require an extended period of time to implement are typically planned as projects at this point. Common culprits for follow-on projects include implementing new high-tech equipment or information systems to create better alignment and enterprise enablement. But really any change that is expected to take significantly longer than the other main parts of the rollout should be planned as individual projects with clearly identified stakeholders from impacted areas participating actively and reporting to a project lead (often the Interim).

EXECUTE ORGANIZATIONAL TRANSFORMATION

With plans in place, the focus now turns to execution. Executing large-scale organizational change often consumes all resources in a company as it transitions to a new and more capable state. This is where the value of quality and detailed planning pays off, helping keep teams focused, and providing concrete reference points and baselines by which progress can be measured.

During all phases, an Interim is typically coaching and teaching other leaders and key resources in the company the tools he or she is using to find, understand, and fix problems in the business. During the execution phase, Interims tend to exhibit relative calm in the face of inevitable challenges. In these instances, they lead by example by showing the rest of the leadership team best practices to assess unplanned or adverse outcomes and replan in real-time. Throughout this process, the leadership team is learning additional skills, gaining knowledge, and using new tools to enable the company to gain traction through alignment of critical assets.

Case Study: Aligning Operational and Revenue Capacity

In 2015 an Interim COO was engaged to help a custom manufacturing company. The company had a sales growth goal of nearly 100 percent year over year. One of the first questions asked by the Interim was "How many items can we currently make?" The executive team members looked a little surprised by this question as they were solely focused on aspects of sales that would need to change to meet their aggressive goal. It was simply assumed that all production and fulfillment processes would scale as needed.

In assessing the feasibility of this goal, the Interim examined the company's manufacturing functions and supporting assets. He learned that the current manufacturing processes were tapped out and could not scale further without major reinvention. The Interim assessed the space, equipment, and end-to-end process efficiency, as well as the alignment of people to their job functions and placement of job functions throughout the company, learning the following:

- There was a poor definition of roles within the production department, reducing efficiency and clouding error tracking to person or task
- The current organization of production resources was based on each process step, resulting in wasted time as people waited for items to reach their station
- Errors frequently reached the last step in the process without being discovered
- The physical plant could only support a single production line; therefore, once production processes were optimized, no additional volume could be accommodated at that facility
- Production yield was approximately 50 percent of what was believed possible based on current team, tools, and approaches
- The current production approach required a complete team of individuals, each with specialized skills, with little cross-training
- Many items moved backward through the process, requiring rework of errors before reaching completion
- Leadership and communication were weak overall with many process problems going unresolved

As the production team was already near capacity at its current process, it became clear to all that doubling sales volume would create serious problems for the company if production capacity and quality was not addressed. The Interim suggested some game-changing approaches and worked with the head of production and CEO to reorganize the company around new ways of manufacturing. Once the plan was ready, it was clearly communicated to the organization, tweaked based on feedback, and executed.

The team switched from a traditional assembly line to an agile development approach that allowed teams of three workers to be accountable for starting and completing a given number of units each day. The production of each unit required several days due to the overall number and complexity of individual steps as well as wait times required to dry or cure glues, fillers, and finishes. The major process steps provided a framework that kept the team focused on getting items to known completion stages each day. Working as a team, quality errors were spotted early, and strategies were developed while working out the problems to avoid repeats. Daily stand-up huddles were instituted where each team member could be positively acknowledged for sharing issues and challenges from the previous day. Some upgrades in equipment were undertaken as it was discovered that bottlenecks were occurring at steps where, with minimal investment, more capable equipment could be employed.

The plan also established go-forward clarity in several regards. After three months of working the new plan, production plans were dialed in to reflect a model that assigned a complexity value to each unit being produced, resulting in a target production schedule of 108 labor hours per week for the team. By using agile methodologies, the company determined it could add a second three-person agile team to the factory working in tandem with the first team, allowing it to double output before running out of capacity, if needed. The company also had clarity on some additional equipment improvements that could be made to aid production in smaller ways as volume grew.

The company broke out parts procurement and quality control functions, and established a new role for these items, creating more production capacity within the team while also establishing accountability for accuracy, parts availability, and final quality inspection tasks. All of these changes ensured continual improvement. The company also learned that the production team was being hampered by a lack of leadership from the production manager, a problem solved by promoting one of the team leaders to lead all production, a welcome change for the team.

The company further improved upstream order entry processes and implemented tools that allowed for more efficient procurement of all of the parts needed for each build and production tracking tools that allowed for data collection at each manufacturing step.

The net results of these organizational changes were as follows:

- Doubled the original production output with the same staff and equipment
- Created ability to scale to four times the original production output by adding a second team of three production workers
- Identified additional productivity enhancing equipment and calculated the anticipated payback to the organization
- Increased production team morale
- Achieved a complete understanding of labor costs at each step, allowing for better definition of product lines and product options, resulting in higher margins

- Removed looming feeling of suddenly outgrowing the current facility
- Rationalized product offerings, eliminating options that created the largest process problems for production and increasing prices for options that could be produced with quality, but which required previously unaccounted-for production time. The result was a more potent and profitable business model.

While optimization and maximization efforts previously allowed the company to create standard processes, these efforts ultimately peaked without further organization of key people, processes, technology, and equipment.

SUMMARY

The final *X-Formation* discipline, organization, adds power to strategy by aligning major resources around the accomplishment of a bold vision, paying dividends by supersizing returns on optimization and maximization efforts. While many organizations and executives focus mainly on organizing people to accomplish important goals, Interims take a full view of all of the company's assets to drive complete results utilizing all of these important investments.

Experienced Interims practice all four *X-Formation* transformation disciplines, trading between each as needs and opportunities become clear, focusing on items with the highest payback in the shortest time to execute first.

SECTION 3

ENGAGING AN INTERIM

Section 1 provided an overview of Interim leadership and what organizations should expect from an Interim. It detailed the characteristics that define successful Interims, situations where an Interim should be considered, and ways Interims start quickly and create significant value.

Section 2 detailed the tools and approaches Interims use to create results time and time again by employing four key *X-Formation* disciplines: strategizing change opportunities, optimizing bottom-line performance, maximizing revenue growth and organizing for totality of results. They further Assess, Plan, and Execute (APE) repeatedly to solve challenges, move the business forward, and lock in gains.

Section 3 will outline the specifics of what to do once you know, or suspect, you have the need for an Interim, including:

Preparing for an Interim—Preparation is key when engaging an Interim. Defining needs and setting goals and parameters for the engagement and preparing the company for the ultimate arrival are all important steps to attaining the greatest results. Chapter 9 discusses these factors as well as preparing for the exit of an Interim throughout the assignment.

Assessing Fit—Each Interim is an individual with different strengths and experiences. Therefore, assessing the skills of a specific individual to a company's needs is an important step in finding the right Interim for a given assignment. Chapter 10 outlines a structured approach that focuses on actual data collected from thousands of Interims and assignment opportunities to detail the factors that need to be assessed to find the right candidate.

When Interims Don't Fit—Despite the many situations where Interims provide exceptional value to a company, this is not always the case. Chapter 11 outlines some specific instances where Interim Executive leadership may not be the best course of action.

How to Find and Engage an Interim—Interims tend to be high-performing individual contributors who oftentimes are presented with opportunities from within their trusted network, as compared to being seen as available in more public or well-established search venues. Chapter 12 outlines methods for locating an Interim Executive and the process of engaging one.

CHAPTER 9

PREPARE

GETTING READY FOR AN INTERIM

As Section 1 established, Interim Executives can help organizations in many ways using specialized skills and deep domain experience. Section 2 detailed how Interims typically go about understanding the needs of the clients and the techniques involved in planning and executing meaningful transformation. With the breadth and depth of opportunities discussed in these sections and numerous factors involved, preparing for an Interim is tantamount to maximizing the value the organization reaps from engaging an external professional executive.

ASSESS NEEDS

Interims hit the ground running and look to address the most pressing issues while preparing the organization for its successor. While Interims use structured approaches like those outlined in Section 2 to assess each client and draw their own conclusions, every company considering Interim Executive leadership should start by stating its highest priority needs and articulating the underlying reasons why it feels it will benefit from the help of an Interim. Using a critical eye on its current performance and opportunities to determine a list of needs, every company should create an up-front list of its most pressing needs.

The framework outlined in Section 2 shows repeated processes for Assessing needs, developing Plans and Executing changes (APE). These factors, therefore, can be used by any company as a framework for evaluating its current performance and highest needs. In cases where a sudden executive need is foisted upon a company, there is often little time for in-depth preparation before interviewing Interim candidates. These situations typically arise due to the sudden departure of a sitting executive, serious illness of an executive or family member, maternity or military leave, or board directives requiring specialization that the company does not possess. Regardless of circumstances, the best Interim engagements start with clarity from the company itself on its needs based on as much forethought as possible.

DEFINE GOALS

Once needs are defined, goals must be set. A common model for setting goals is to use the acronym SMART as defined by its creator George T. Doran:[15]

> **Specific**—Use action words (e.g. develop, design, create) to describe the goal
>
> **Measurable**—Use objective data (dollars, units, percentages, etc.) to measure results
>
> **Acceptable**—Gain consensus with all stakeholders of the priority and need for the goal
>
> **Realistic**—Ensure the goal is challenging but attainable with no major barriers
>
> **Time-Bound**—Set a specific time frame by when the goal must be accomplished

An example of a well-stated goal is "Reduce the cost of goods by 10 percent for the last six months of this fiscal year without adversely impacting the quality of the products or requiring capital investment of more than $50,000." While this exercise may seem sophomoric, goal setting in this fashion is considered a best practice and widely used by companies

---

15 George T. Doran, "There's a S.M.A.R.T. Way to Write Management's Goals and Objectives." *Management Review* (November 1981): 35–36.

that over perform. It is surprising how many companies fail to define goals in a manner in which it can be shared, validated, measured, and accurately assessed for completion.

For each of the needs defined, at least one goal should be developed. Some needs may require several goals from different individuals or departments in order to satisfy the need. For example, a need to address a product gap in the marketplace may require goals from engineering, marketing, sales, and service.

Each goal should be written down and approved by the executive team, CEO, and the board if appropriate. Once concretely defined, these goals become helpful during the recruiting process as they will define the skillset needed for the Interim. They will also allow the Interim and the company to align on the scope and timing of the assignment and provide clarity to the executive team on any skillset gaps it will need an Interim to fill.

It should be noted that many organizations that engage Interims are not in a position to set specific goals for an Interim to accomplish because the executive team simply does not know what to expect or it does not understand the nature of the issues it is experiencing. In these instances, Interims will typically share similar situations they have encountered and the path forward as they see it to help the set initial expectations. Once the assignment begins, common goals are created as the facts become clear.

SET PARAMETERS

Interims arrive on the job focused on achieving meaningful results, ready to take the reins of the organization and make decisions and drive the company forward. While Interims serve as deeply trusted advisors to their clients, they are not on board to consult. They assume the organization is prepared to fund initiatives and move quickly. Defining the parameters of the engagement before recruiting the Interim is essential to ensuring a good match, establishing a common understanding of the scope of the assignment, and setting the stage for execution. Some key questions each company should answer include:

> **How Much?** A budget for the engagement should be prepared. Quite often the Interim will be commuting for the position and will need a hotel, car, and meal or per diem reimbursement in addition to the fee for his or her services. While straight fee-based compensation is the norm, many engagements include incentives, an equity stake in the company, or other forms of alternate compensation. All factors impacting the budget and compensation should be discussed up-front to ensure that qualified Interims can be appropriately filtered.
>
> **How Often?** This question includes two important facets. The first is the frequency with which the company expects the Interim to work on its initiatives. The second is the duration or effort that will accompany that

frequency. Some Interim engagements are full time for a stated duration. In these instances, the amount of anticipated effort comprising full time should be considered. Some Interim engagements are fractional, meaning the Interim will work less than full time for the client. In these situations, expectations and budget should be clear in establishing the effort and frequency of an Interim's involvement. Similarly, if remote working scenarios are part of the engagement, then expectations for offsite and onsite work should be established. Periodic review of the Interim's progress is essential, so the company should also define the schedule and method for reporting updates to the CEO or board before an engagement begins.

How Much Authority? A key to the Interim's effectiveness is his or her ability and willingness to exercise judgment on many matters without needing to formally ask the board or other top executives for permission. If the Interim will be approving expenditures, investments, or other financial matters, then a table should be developed that outlines the signing authority. Define how much latitude the Interim has in changing processes, procedures, and culture without checking in with the board. Often, a not-to-exceed provision is useful in outlining important boundaries.

For How Long? It is important to define the length of

the engagement and whether it is for a fixed duration or dependent upon the completion of key milestones up front. For assignments where the duration may be unclear or unknown until further assessment is performed and plans are created, the client should consider stating a general timeline with predefined check-in dates. Programs like InterimExecs Rapid Executive Deployment (RED) provide a predefined framework and time frame for assessing a company's needs and presenting a go-forward plan at a fixed price.

For What Outcome? An Interim can be engaged for a wide range of tasks. Perhaps filling in until a new CEO is hired while making minimal changes is all that is needed. For some major engagements the Interim may be asked to recruit new executives and rebuild complete teams. Other situations may require the Interim to raise capital or sell the company. In every case, the scope of the desired outcome should be well-defined and documented so the organization and the Interim are aligned from day one.

The greater the forethought on the specifics of its needs, the faster the process of locating the right Interim will proceed for an organization once the search begins.

ASSIGN AN APPROPRIATE TITLE AND POSITION

Care should be taken to give the Interim the necessary level of authority and accountability to accomplish the goals outlined and presented during the recruiting process. If the Interim is replacing the CEO, then "Interim CEO" is an appropriate title. It is imperative that the organization understands the Interim is in charge and will be making decisions that must be implemented, and that "Interim" does not mean "Powerless."

This distinction is especially important in situations where the search for a permanent executive is occurring during the Interim's tenure. In these situations, the existing executive team, and the organization at large, will need to embrace and support what may appear to be a confusing and threatening situation. Some of the current executives may be threatened by the sudden appearance of a powerful and unknown peer or superior, while some may want to be considered for the open position and misunderstand that the Interim is not necessarily in place because there are no good internal candidates. In these situations, the decision-makers who engaged the Interim should decide early on if internal candidates will be considered and how the search process will be conducted.

There are many reasons that those in the organization may be inclined initially to view the Interim's arrival as less than positive and be disinclined to participate fully in *X-formation* activities. Key employees wanting to be in step and in favor with the new top executive may also hold back in working with the Interim. They may not want to spend time getting to know a lame duck or start on a new project when feeling that the new executive will probably change it anyway. Further, some employees may use the need for change as an opportunity to seek employment at a new company where there is more perceived certainty.

In all of these situations, it is important for the decision-makers and executive team to focus on the anticipated benefits, framing the change positively, with excitement and a focus on opportunity. Interims are experts at helping craft and deliver these messages as these skills are required at most, if not all, of their engagements, and they should be relied on to help in this regard.

> It is imperative that the organization understands the Interim is in charge and will be making decisions that must be implemented. "Interim" does not mean "Powerless."

PREPARE YOUR TEAM

When organizations choose to bring in an Interim rather than a permanent replacement, there will be questions from the executives and staff. To head off disruptive rumors, the organization needs to be proactive and message the news in a timely and positive manner.

The board (or the CEO if the Interim is a lesser C-level executive) should prepare and deliver a compelling case for why an Interim Executive is being brought into the organization. Successfully delivering this message will provide the organization with an understanding of the framework and context of what to expect during the coming months, will create a positive impression of the Interim as a resource engaged to help, and will serve as a guidepost for the work to be performed. The most compelling arguments use data and logic to lay out specific needs and goals of the company as well as parameters of the assignment, in line with the vision, mission, and core values of the company.

Typical questions asked by the staff and other executives include:

> **Why an Interim?** In addressing this question, the company should be clear on the value it sees in using an Interim, sharing supporting points in a consistent manner, such as:

- Interim Executives have become an effective alternative to using a consultant or leaving a position vacant while a search for the right person is conducted.
- Interims help bring a fresh, unbiased review of the factors driving operational results.
- An Interim will bring specialized skills and experience in solving similar challenges at other companies, not to mention a track record of success.

- An Interim does not waste time or company resources trying to secure a full-time job but instead is driven by the opportunity to make changes that lead to a sustainable value increase for all business stakeholders.
- The company should expect immediate improvement in delivery quality and cost while a search is conducted to fill the permanent position.

Who Will Report to the Interim? The Interim will usually have the same direct reports as the outgoing executive unless there is a reason to restructure. One reason for a different reporting structure may be limitations of the previous executive, while another may be splitting one large role into two as regularly happens as companies scale up and out. In some scenarios, it may make sense to reduce the number of subordinates in order to obtain a tighter focus on some key areas. Regardless of the situation, it is imperative that the organization know both provisional and future reporting structure. If part of the Interim's role is to evaluate and suggest a future structure, care should be taken to explain this in a way that does not create panic in the team.

How to Communicate to the Staff? While the decision-maker(s) engaging an Interim are normally enthusiastic and optimistic about the results to be obtained, care should always be taken to create positive messages that emphasize solving problems and articulate expected benefits. Communications should state the company's needs and goals, as well as parameters which led to the decision to bring in an Interim. Messaging should include specific skills the Interim possesses that directly map to the company's needs, instilling confidence in all that this newcomer to the organization will add skills and experience that do not exist in-house. Obviously, in some situations there may be a need to hold back some sensitive issues until the Interim has been able to make a clear assessment and review it with the board of directors.

FORMAL INTRODUCTION

Once an Interim has been engaged, the direct reports and other key employees should be brought together in a meeting for the introduction of the Interim. The reasons for hiring the Interim should be reviewed along with the key areas of focus. The Interim should be given the floor to present a background overview and answer any questions. Each staff member present should also review his or her function(s), tenure with the company, and background. This serves as an ice-breaker meeting and initiates an open dialog for the future.

After the meeting, an all-employee announcement regarding the Interim's arrival must be sent, which might look like:

Staff,

As you know we are engaged in the search for a new [executive role/title]. While we conduct this search, we want to continue our progress toward our mission of [state summary of company mission]. To ensure we stay on track, we have asked [Interim's name] to fill in as an Interim [executive role/title] until a permanent executive is onboard.

In addition to [#] years of real-world executive leadership experience in [name the domain], [Interim's name] has successfully helped many companies achieve their goals. As an expert in [list skills like startups, turnarounds, acquisition integration, M&A, financing, business development, process innovation, etc.], we feel the company will greatly benefit from [his/her] knowledge and skills. [Interim's name] will have the same responsibility and authority, and should be viewed in the same light, as a permanent executive in this position even though [Interim's name] will not be a permanent employee of the company.

[His/Her] responsibilities will include:

1. Working with the executive team to provide guidance and leadership toward our goals and objectives
2. Identifying new opportunities for growth and profitability

3. Assisting the recruiting team in evaluating and selecting the new [executive role/title]

    Feel free to meet with [Interim's name] at your earliest convenience to see where [he/she] may be of help to you. These are exciting times for our company. We appreciate your continued support and ask that you work proactively and cooperatively with [Interim's name] to keep the momentum going for our business.

    Respectfully,

    [The Management Team/BOD/CEO/etc.]

Immediately after the message is sent, the Interim should schedule one-on-one meetings with the direct reports for a more detailed discussion to be followed by an introduction to their staff in each department. This will reduce anxiety and give the Interim an opportunity to become acquainted firsthand with the team, as well as answer any further questions regarding the assignment. These initial meetings often mark the start of the assessment process.

SUMMARY

The involvement of an Interim can be surprising to an organization. Therefore, a company should prepare for an Interim by clearly identifying its needs and goals prior to starting a search. The company should define parameters for the assignment, including scope, budget, weekly effort, anticipated duration, and reporting structure. Once this written scope of work is approved by the CEO and board, the recruiting process can begin using these factors to discuss the assignment with candidates.

Planning for an Interim should extend through activities required to introduce the new leader to the organization. The company should use the entrance of an Interim to clearly communicate its goals to the organization and succinctly state the value proposition for this approach. Creating a positive and smooth introduction of the new leader to the company is a critical first step in creating strong relationships and realizing the value the Interim is to deliver.

CHAPTER 10

ASSESS

FINDING THE RIGHT INTERIM TO FIT YOUR NEEDS

Assessing the specific skills and experience of an Interim as compared to the requirements of a given engagement is a critical step in the process, for both parties. A client is looking for assurance that the Interim will be able to provide game-changing results by successfully achieving stated goals within a target time frame and budget, and making the inevitable tough calls necessary to guide leaders through sometimes difficult situations. Interims, on the other hand, are evaluating the organization's overall willingness to embrace change, realism of plans and expectations, likely resources available, existence of sacred cows or artificial barriers, and other indications that the company may not be ready for *X-Formation*.

Each Interim inevitably uses his or her own process for gauging overall fit and the likelihood that meaningful value can be added. Experienced Interims have been through this process many times and typically lead the client through the decision points and utilize skills such as active listening to create a common understanding of needs and constraints. When a particular Interim proves to not be a solid fit for a given opportunity, that person will often suggest an introduction to another Interim who may be a better fit given the company's specific needs.

For a company engaging an Interim, particularly if it has not done so previously, the process of evaluating the Interim's ability to help it can seem uncertain and even daunting, requiring consideration of a large number of factors. Fortunately, through a great deal of experience and study, a framework has been developed that can be used to accurately assess an Interim's fit.

InterimExecs, the premier membership organization for practicing Interims, applied deduction and logic to this challenge using data from interviews with thousands of potential Interims and countless clients to develop a repeatable process for evaluating the skills of an Interim. In helping companies capitalize on opportunities and surmount their specific challenges, InterimExecs produced this structured framework for assessing the Interim-client-opportunity fit across nine specific areas of experience and personality. The details of this framework are presented here, in *X-Formation*, to the public for the first time.

The InterimExecs Best Fit Match Matrix outlines nine key areas of alignment that ultimately form the basis for measuring an individual's fit to a given opportunity. These dynamics, ranked by increasing importance, are:

1. **Industry**—Industries worked and roles held
2. **Location**—Proximity of company to Interim's home
3. **Skills**—Specific domain expertise or required knowledge or experience
4. **Stage**—Size and age of company
5. **Wins**—Experience in similar successful *X-Formation* situations
6. **Behavior**—Attitude of both parties, specifically in relation to the task at hand
7. **Values**—Character, as demonstrated through past experience and accomplishments
8. **Mindset**—Can-do attitude and willingness to enter the danger
9. **Chemistry**—Feeling of both parties that company, opportunity, and Interim are well aligned

While Interim engagements typically have short exit clauses that allow for flexibility if results are not as either side would expect, it is no less important to go through a formal evaluation of how a specific Interim can address the specific needs of the organization while working cooperatively with other executives and staff.

> InterimExecs has discovered that only about 2 percent of applicants qualify for membership to its organization using its assessment of skills and experience, the Best Fit Match Matrix.

It is important to know that not all Interims are created equal. As discussed in Chapter 3: "Pedigree," true Interims lead organizations from within, crave change and transformation, and bring skills required for outstanding executive leadership. Since the notion of what an Interim is (or isn't) has been loosely defined to date, many accomplished people fashion themselves Interims, despite not having proven competency in all skills required to deliver value in these challenging roles. Therefore, an owner or board of directors could easily be led astray by an executive who believes he or she possesses the proper skills, while not actually having the track record to know. In setting the bar as such, InterimExecs has discovered that only about 2 percent of applicants qualify for membership using its assessment of skills and experience within this scoring framework.

InterimExecs Best Fit Match Matrix

		CHEMISTRY	BEST FIT!
	VALUES	MINDSET	WHY?
STAGE	WINS	BEHAVIOR	HOW?
INDUSTRY	LOCATION	SKILLS	WHAT?

The InterimExecs Best Fit Match Matrix organizes the nine key areas of alignment, looking at each level with varying importance, culminating with the holy grail: chemistry. The remainder of this chapter outlines these nine key areas of alignment, their importance, and how to utilize each to assess fit.

BEST FIT LEVEL 1: WHAT?

INDUSTRY

The first question many companies ask is whether or not an Interim Executive has experience in his/her industry. In reality, prior experience in a specific industry may be a positive benefit or a drawback. Industry-specific experience is a positive when the vast accumulation of knowledge from prior roles instantly becomes relevant in a new situation, crisis, or opportunity. This is especially true in navigating highly regulated industries such as healthcare, insurance, finance, and banking.

Sometimes, however, all the accumulated wisdom can backfire, especially in industries facing significant transformation.

In these instances, fresh thinking is mandatory. Executives who have spent an entire career in one given industry often become entrenched in stale approaches, suffering from limited perspectives. A hallmark of many successful Interims is having demonstrated success across several different industries. This cross-pollination helps them understand the limitations and strengths of given tools and approaches when applied in different ways, enabling the Interim to speak from varied experience in helping future clients assess complex situations and opportunities.

An important advantage the Interim Executive brings to a client is fresh thinking and third-party objectivity. In most cases, all of the industry expertise that is needed is already within the company. Good Interims use great facilitation skills to draw out solutions while also introducing best practices from experience gained by working with many different types of companies. Quality Interims draw others into the discussion and discovery process by asking them to share the expertise and insights, not by ruling in dictatorial fashion, barking out orders or acting in know-it-all fashion.

The job of an Interim is to ask the right questions, actively listen to those within the company, and facilitate the process of drawing out solutions from the team while developing the go-forward plan. When roadblocks are discovered and specialized experience is needed, the Interim will find the right people for the job. When an InterimExecs RED Team member recently stepped into a shuttered, family-owned manufacturing company in California, he drew on expertise within the company to solve a massive water issue and get the boilers back up and running. "You don't walk in knowing all the answers," he said. "The people who are doing this for years may not have the perfect answer, but they have been watching it and see what is successful." It is, therefore, important that companies look at an Interim's skills and experience solving similar challenges and achieving meaningful results that match that company's goals, and not simply work performed in that industry.

LOCATION

> Close proximity does not guarantee highest quality. Quality counts for much more than random geography.

When considering the proximity of an Interim to a specific opportunity as a decision-making criterion, the perspective of *Tribes* author Seth Godin should be considered.[16] Godin admonishes to never eat sushi at the airport, proposing that simply because one may get off a plane and have a craving for sushi does not mean that person should stop ten feet from the gate to buy the sushi that is closest at hand. Close proximity does not guarantee highest quality, and the same thinking applies to Interims. Quality counts for much more than random geography.

16 Seth Godin, *Tribes: We Need You to Lead Us* (London: Penguin Books, 2008).

Many company owners and investors considering Interim assistance are doing so for the first time. With limited knowledge of the differences between a permanent search and an Interim search, they may easily default to thinking that an Interim must be located close to the office or plant, or must relocate. This is a flawed approach. Location should be at the bottom of the list when securing a great Interim Executive. Many Interims travel the world to take on great challenges and have the frequent-flier miles to prove it. Because of the short-term nature of assignments, they rarely, if ever, permanently relocate. Instead, they go to the problem, challenge, or opportunity. This involves commuting to the company headquarters, finding temporary housing, or working virtually. Each situation is unique and is dependent on the needs of the company, but the key is looking for best-fit talent.

As the world becomes smaller through video conferencing and online meeting tools, and as the trends toward outsourcing, offshoring, and remote contractor help expands, many Interims have started working engagements using a remote approach. Companies with severe budget constraints may explore an engagement where the Interim spends, say, one week on site and one week working remotely. Since the pool of high quality Interim talent worldwide is limited, constraining the search by geography may result in a longer search to find the right Interim, so utilizing remote working approaches can significantly expand the pool of candidates.

SKILLS

The skills of an Interim Executive include both that person's experience across various functions (e.g. sales, operations, marketing, finance, and accounting) within different organizations, and also the accumulated wisdom, methodologies, and track record that person brings to bear in a given engagement.

One of the biggest stumbling blocks for company owners is recognizing the difference between skills and industry experience. It is easy to believe that an executive who has spent considerable time in a particular industry will be better equipped to enter another company in the same industry. Sometimes that is true, but not necessarily. Industry experience is not the same thing as skill-building or as having a solid track record delivering meaningful results.

Consider a hypothetical example: Executive A spent his entire career in the automotive industry. Executive B had increasing levels of authority in the automotive industry plus two other industries before becoming an Interim. Executive B typically proves over time to be the better Interim. Cross-pollination from various industries serves to do two things: first, it creates a well-rounded executive who learned different operating systems at different companies in different industries; and second, it provides a solid baseline that shows the executive's range of capability and accomplishments in situations requiring different skills.

Standard résumés paint with very broad strokes regarding an Interim's qualifications, but typically add few meaningful insights that aid a company's search. Interviews, however, afford the opportunity for mutual evaluation of compatibility, allowing the company to share its goals and challenges, while also providing the Interim with the opportunity to relate past accomplishments to those needs. Companies, therefore, should focus on transferable skills, such as the process of taking a company public, bringing about operational or supply chain improvements, expanding into international markets, preparing for an audit, or similar broad objectives the company perceives the Interim will need to surmount. These explorations enable the client to reveal what needs to get done and determine if the Interim has the ability to learn quickly to accomplish set goals.

BEST FIT LEVEL 2: HOW?

STAGE

Have you ever met someone who specializes in turnarounds? That person has a very different mindset from, say, an executive or entrepreneur who thrives in startups. The turnaround executive is oriented toward fixing problems and eliminating barriers to profitability and stability: How do we save assets? What can we trim? The startup executive has a completely different outlook, one oriented toward questions like: How do we turn this acorn into a mighty oak tree? How do we go from zero to one billion dollars in revenue? How can we build a great long-term team? Or, how can we be first to market?

Companies go through many different life cycle stages such as launch, scaling up into new markets, organic growth, expansion through acquisitions, turnaround, and ultimately exit (whether sale, IPO, or merger). Each stage requires a different cadence, mindset, and skillset. Companies should look for similarities between their current stage and experiences the Interim has had at other companies. Many executives have a sweet spot—a stage that they love jumping into—where they ramp up fastest and ultimately perform highest.

WINS

"Winning isn't everything, it's the only thing."

—VINCE LOMBARDI

There is a certain ineffable quality to a winner. Tom Brady. Sara Blakely. Warren Buffett. Oprah Winfrey. Steve Jobs. In all fields of endeavor there tend to be standout winners who accomplish the biggest goals, tackle the most daunting problems, and ultimately have more wins, demonstrating excellence time after time. Who is that winning leader for your company?

Interims, as a class, represent executives who accomplish meaningful results in difficult circumstances, repeatedly.

It has to be this way with the best Interims, otherwise, they could not be entrusted to take on responsibility to lead a company, division, or important project through a meaningful *X-Formation* and into unfamiliar territory.

Interims make their living by going into organizations for short periods of time, doing well and delivering success. Those who cannot repeatedly produce results quickly tend to struggle, ultimately deciding they are not cut out for a career in Interim Executive leadership. Permanent executives can settle in and stay in roles for many, many years, building familiarity with the requirements of that specific role at one particular company. Many prefer the safety of an established company, often learning the skills necessary for stability and staying out of the crosshairs as compared to those required to continually innovate. Executives of this class who try Interim work, typically find it too chaotic and demanding as they struggle to quickly adapt to rapidly changing environments where soft leadership skills like coaching others are frequently as important as hard leadership skills like budgeting or creating a technical architecture.

Interims do not have the luxury of settling into an easy pace in a comfortable environment. They use proven approaches and keen intuition to thrive in fast-paced environments where markets and technology are evolving, innovation is needed, or new thinking is essential for survival. Since these scenarios provide little in the way of excess time or consideration for whether or not things are working, Interims tend to sink or swim after a few assignments. Any company considering engaging an Interim should look at that candidate's track record of success and tangible wins to confirm that the Interim is qualified.

MINDSET

Why do you do what you do? We all have a why that drives us. InterimExecs uses a detailed process that helps it understand the why behind the most successful Interims in the world. This assessment is vital in weeding out people who may be looking at Interim assignments as a way to a full-time job, those who are more interested in a paycheck than having major impact, or individuals who simply misunderstand the full scope of depth and breadth of skills required to be successful as an Interim.

In some ways, the new specialty of Interim Executive leadership goes against every notion of traditional employment. Human Resources (HR) managers seek consistency and commonality. Interim Executives are not individuals who try a job out by first calling them "Interim" as they evaluate if they would like the position long-term. An Interim, flashing a traditional résumé showing project after project at company after company, would be pegged as a job hopper or potentially even incompetent by traditional HR specialists. Of course, these observations would be inaccurate and could not be further from the truth. Interims choose this career and lifestyle, craving the recurring cycle of starting new engagements and moving on as soon as objectives are attained. Great Interims are routinely asked by client companies to become a permanent member of the Executive Team. When posed with this question, the answer is generally something like, "No, but thank you. I'm flattered that you feel my presence here has been so valuable."

Why would someone give up the stability of a full-time job for short assignments, especially knowing that most assignments are messy, require being on the road, and dealing with dysfunctional organizations and individuals? It boils down to mindset. Interims love challenge and change. They are excellent at stepping into a company at a critical turning point and leading it successfully through the fog, while being unexcited by running things that are smooth and steady for the long haul. To a true Interim, the stakes matter, and if the stakes are not high, then it just is not as rewarding.

On the short end, an Interim may go into a company for a few months. On the long end it may be for a few years, especially if the assignment is working for a private equity portfolio or is an organization that is growing to the point of exit. If an executive says that he wants the interim assignment as a try-to-buy situation, or would be open to interim or full-time work, then that person is probably a permanent executive in disguise looking to assess long-term fit and not a true Interim who is looking to transform the company.

BEST FIT LEVEL 3: WHY?

VALUES

It goes without saying that a successful leader must have integrity, and yet, this underlying core principle is not universal. One need look no further than today's news to see examples of leaders betraying trust or undermining their own organizations. Integrity is a condition of wholeness and is demonstrated by Interims daily by honoring his or her word, being honest and up-front with everyone (especially the executive team and board), staying true to an organization's highest principles, and operating in a transparent manner.

Speaking truth to power is a common Interim principal and an excellent example of how Interims maintain integrity in even the most difficult circumstances. If integrity is lacking on the part of the leader, then building trust becomes impossible as others doubt that person's motives, intentions, and inevitably, that person's ability to do the right thing.

> Interims view dysfunction in a different light than employees, knowing that misalignment, distrust, or dishonesty at the top of an organization will make it impossible to achieve lasting results.

The best Interims provide value up front (before any contract is signed) by freely sharing their insights and acting with integrity by protecting confidential information as they discuss *X-Formations* they successfully led. Because Interims routinely enter troubled environments, and have seen firsthand the mess created by companies bogged down with fraudulent situations or dishonesty amongst the previous management team, they quickly establish transparency and work hard to maintain it.

Interims view dysfunction in a different light than employees, knowing that misalignment, distrust, or dishonesty at the top of an organization will make it impossible to achieve lasting results. Permanent employees can often become entangled in corporate politics, trying to please the powers that be to keep their jobs secure. When determining the fit of a particular Interim, it is important to have confidence that person will do the right thing in difficult situations and advocate for what is in the best interest of the company. Especially if it means speaking unpleasant truths. Chapter 11: "Misalignment," outlines situations where engaging an Interim may not be the best option for a company. For instance, organizations that are not willing to address areas of dysfunction head-on are examples of those that would have difficulty getting long-term results from an Interim's involvement.

BEHAVIOR

We each have an instinctive and intuitive way we perform work. One Interim describes himself as a sprinter rather than a marathon runner. Another focuses much of his time empowering those around him to take responsibility, continually creating self-sufficiency so the company will hardly notice his departure at the end of the assignment. Understanding how an Interim would approach your assignment is key in assessing if that person is a good fit for your company's *X-Formation* needs.

Focused interview questions can tell a lot about how quickly an Interim Executive will ramp up and how that person will work. These could include: When you begin an assignment, what do you do on day one? What does your process for assessing a company in our current situation look like? Or, how do you evaluate if a company has the right executive team to accomplish its plans?

Often described as conative fit, companies can formally measure the mode in which Interims approach their work through tests like the Kolbe Profile. These assessments focus on how individuals view work and relationships, providing insights that can be used to form teams with complementary strengths in various work modes.

Entrepreneurs, for example, tend to have a dominant Kolbe trait called "Quick Start" in which they have an ability to make fast decisions with very little information. A financial analyst, on the other hand, could exhibit the Kolbe trait of being a high "Fact Finder", preferring to dig into details and perform analytics.

Each Interim tends to have some go-to tools and approaches that he or she will use in starting assignments, executing initiatives, and dealing with adversity. These could best be described as habits. When assessing fit, companies are well advised to ask about the tools or approaches the Interim candidate has used in similar situations, the results delivered, and how he or she would approach the *X-Formation* given the client's situation.

Understanding an Interim's work mode can be helpful to the legacy team as it processes how this newcomer to the organization normally operates. While this is clearly an important factor in assessing the overall fit of an Interim to a specific role and company, care should be taken by an organization not to be swayed from an otherwise strong fit because of unfamiliarity with the Interim's work style. Remember, Interims bring vastly different approaches to their clients and often provide game-changing insights and concepts to transform the way problems are approached and solved. These approaches are rooted in past success but may seem unnatural to companies, especially in the beginning of the engagement.

CHEMISTRY

The final aspect of fit is chemistry. Chemistry is the difficult-to-measure feeling and attraction that is created between a company, its executive team and a prospective Interim. Decision-makers for the client as well as the Interim should all feel positive chemistry forming as discussion occurs related to the company, its needs, and the Interim's experience.

Interactions that seem forced, points that are repeatedly misunderstood, or areas of contention all point to misalignment between the Interim and the client's needs. Organizations searching for an Interim should be wary of thinking focused too tightly on finding the perfect candidate and instead encourage open-mindedness in painting the picture of a better and more prosperous future for all. Sometimes chemistry carries the day, being that final positive gut feeling that causes executive teams to accept a given Interim as part of their team.

In situations where chemistry does not feel right, there may be some underlying issue, baggage, or mind trash that is preventing this final positive feeling. Organizations looking for Interim Executive assistance need to be honest and transparent in discussing the challenges with any candidate. Elephants in the room or other caginess on behalf of the company in sharing its challenges honestly will ultimately conspire to create strange chemistry as the Interim struggles to understand what the true needs of that potential client entail.

Once there is a meeting of the minds, the deployment process begins by creating a scope of work for the assignment, negotiating fees, and drawing up a contract, topics covered in Chapter 12.

SUMMARY

Through analysis of valuable data collected over thousands of interviews with Interims and clients, and decades of experience placing Interims in engagements, InterimExecs has created a repeatable framework that should be used by all organizations in assessing the fit of a particular Interim to their specific needs.

This Best Fit Match Matrix identifies nine key areas of alignment (dynamics) that, together, assess the fit of a specific Interim to a given opportunity. It organizes each area of potential consideration in order of priority, starting with low-grade indicators such as proximity of an Interim to an assignment and ascending to the chemistry that exists between a company and a specific candidate. By using this framework, a company can apply a proven methodology to finding the perfect Interim to address its specific needs.

CHAPTER 11

MISALIGNMENT

WHEN INTERIMS ARE NOT A GOOD OPTION

There are certainly times when engaging an Interim will not be the best solution for a company in need. Sometimes a permanent executive might be the most appropriate solution, but the organization may not be ready to utilize the approaches taken by Interims to address issues quickly. Furthermore, Interims' determination to move quickly, willingness to challenge the status quo, and insistence on transparency can be disruptive to some companies. Scenarios such as these create an even more unproductive environment for companies that are unwilling to embrace the opportunity for fresh thinking and overall transformation. It is for these reasons that any company considering Interim Executive assistance should review the following areas of concern candidly before deciding to hire an Interim.

> It was with shock that the Interim was told by the CEO that he was not interested in executing broad changes to the business in the next six months that would deliver an additional $400,000 annually to the bottom line. The company was hyper-profitable, and the changes outlined were perceived to be potentially painful.

POSITIONS WITHOUT INFLUENCE

To have an impact on a company, an Interim must have the authority to lead the organization and make decisions as would be expected of a respected full-time executive in that position. If an Interim is going to be endowed with less authority than the full-time owner of that role, or otherwise be expected to act in a lesser fashion, then the company should seek other types of assistance.

Interims are change agents who must be empowered with a focused purpose, authority, position and title. Those engaged to accomplish a market basket of tasks across different areas of the business typically do not have proper authority to effectively lead the organization through challenges. Similarly, dotted-line reporting structures without direct accountability and influence create barriers, conflict, and provide little clarity on who has authority to make which decisions.

Therefore, organizations looking for a senior person to accomplish given projects may want to consider a more traditional consultant to work on these initiatives reporting to a permanent executive or properly define a role for an Interim VP of Special Projects. Companies that have executive leaders in place for each function but are looking to grow the skills of those individuals to solve larger problems may want to consider executive coaching. Those looking for help setting strategy may want to consider engaging a strategist or facilitator who can help the executive team to workshop the necessary missing components.

Regardless of the circumstances, situations where Interims are engaged to address needs without the corresponding authority, title, or the same expectation of leadership that a permanent executive would provide in that same role should be avoided as this is a warning sign of misunderstanding of how an Interim operates and are unlikely to succeed.

ORGANIZATIONS WITH STRONG LEADERSHIP TEAMS

Interims are first and foremost leaders. Companies with a fully staffed executive team, therefore, are not prepared to benefit from an Interim's help, nor can an Interim properly help a company without a defined leadership role. Companies without a true Interim need, but which are looking for better results, often benefit from different types of assistance, including hiring business coaches, engaging subject matter experts, and adopting a framework for business operation and excellence, like the Entrepreneurial Operating System®, or Scaling Up©[17] methodologies. Companies requiring specific domain expertise to solve a specific, deep, or complex problem should consider traditional consulting organizations that have demonstrated success in solving similar challenges for their clients.

It should be noted that companies that have a fully-staffed executive team, but which are in the process of scaling up or scaling out, are a different situation. As a company passes significant growth thresholds, it will often need to add new positions to the executive team, or C-suite. These situations represent great opportunities to engage an Interim. For example, at smaller scale, many companies have a combined VP of Sales and Marketing. When the company reaches the stage where it makes sense to separate these roles to gain deeper competency in each individual discipline, the executive in that position will occupy one seat, creating an excellent opportunity for an Interim Executive to fill the other seat. The Interim will guide the organization through adapting to the new function(s), building out the team, creating go-forward strategy and plans, and ultimately helping to hire the full-time executive.

ORGANIZATIONS RESISTANT TO CHANGE

One of the most important characteristics of any organiza-

17 Verne Harnish, *Scaling Up: How a Few Companies Make It...and Why the Rest Don't* (Ashburn, VA: Gazelles, 2014).

tion engaging an Interim is embracing meaningful change and the uncertainty that comes with it. Old barriers and ways of doing business will fall away when new and more advanced approaches are introduced, but only if the change is embraced by the organization and its legacy leadership team. Therefore, a willingness to change is a necessity for an organization to maximize the investment made by engaging an Interim. While it may sound silly, deep down, some organizations and executives are looking for validation and ego stroking as opposed to meaningful *X-Formation.*

Great Interims are also excellent teachers. They create trust by demonstrating their deep understanding of the factors impacting the company and the ways similar challenges have been solved at other companies. Many ideas presented will be considered too radical or otherwise not right for the organization at first, as comfortable and known ways of doing business are presented as barriers to the new ideas. However, an Interim needs to be viewed as a change agent and be both empowered and trusted to lead the organization in new directions, some of which will be foreign and potentially frightening to the company and its leaders.

Willingness to change is one of the foremost characteristics of high-performing companies. Stagnant organizations eventually are faced with challenges they cannot overcome, placing the viability of the company at risk. It is well known that roughly 96 percent of companies fail in a given ten-year period.[18] Established companies and startups alike face challenges that threaten their existence. This phenomenon is known as the evolution-revolution cycle.

Evolutionary cycles occur as companies hit barriers and fail to break through. These organizations introduce refinements to past strategies or tactics in an attempt to obtain the desired results. These tactics provide positive results over time, but eventually are unable to achieve their ultimate goal. Evolutionary approaches are great for making incremental improvements, but are inadequate when major change is needed.

Revolutionary events represent new and innovative approaches that fundamentally change the way business, or parts or it, is addressed. These new methods cause a breakthrough to new heights with barriers that prevented previous progress falling away, creating powerful new ways of doing business.

Interims are regularly seen as the revolutionary agents who foment change and enable progressive outcomes. Interims produce results by introducing business methods that are often provocative, relying on experience to help struggling companies solve problems in new and innovative ways. The best and most innovative approaches will, however, fail to deliver results unless there is a company-wide willingness

18 Bill Carmody, "Why 96% of Businesses Fail within 10 Years," Inc.com, August 12, 2015.

to embrace new ideas and commit to the activities required for *X-Formation*.

NO IMPETUS TO CHANGE

Impetus to change is similar to, but a little different than, an organization's willingness to change. Ideally, a company should be able to articulate an important challenge that needs to be met with the help of an Interim. This is its impetus for change. Great Interims not only embrace change, but view the need for a major change as being critical to their role and ability to be successful.

Therefore, organizations engaging an Interim should identify their most pressing needs prior to selecting an Interim and also be prepared to view the business with fresh eyes and a willingness to change. If no major challenges can be identified, then the company should revisit its desire to utilize an Interim to ensure a clear role exists that is driven by a desire for *X-Formation*.

Case Study: Bottom-Line Breakdown

In 2016 an Interim was engaged by a fast-growing manufacturer of luxury building supplies. This company had an $8 million sales forecast and recently had experienced rapid growth, doubling its sales over the previous two years. With its rapid growth, the company was discovering that it needed to scale up critical roles, especially in operations. The company tried several approaches on its own but had growing quality issues, particularly with in-house processes in the middle part of its supply and value chains. The company manufactured the metal frames outside of the US, with each unit being custom for the job, performing final assembly and installation at its factory in the US.

The assignment was to assess optimization opportunities, firm up operations, and define the role of the COO to determine if the company needed a stronger executive in the position. The noise level from the staff, customers, and management had gotten so high, that the founder and CEO decided to act, engaging the Interim to help him sort out the issues, the needs of the company, and the best path forward. The Interim COO was asked to start by focusing on the in-house manufacturing process. In his first three days, the Interim interviewed the CEO, head of operations, production lead, field installation manager/scheduler, and head of finance. The results painted a picture showing quality issues and operational inefficiencies that started in the sales process and extended through final installation and job completion.

Some specific findings included:

- Poor space utilization, wasting 65 percent of storage capacity
- Handwritten order documents were hampering offshore manufacturing and local installation crews alike
- Large inefficiencies resulted from utilizing two separate facilities in the US for product storage, handling, and finish
- No controls were in place to manage high-cost parts and supplies
- Many installations required rework at a minimum cost of $400 per visit, often requiring several revisits
- Inefficiencies, spotty utilization, and lack of ability to measure cost/benefit of specific actions due to poor role definition, and split focus in critical roles
- Slap-dash decision-making, including signing a

lease for additional warehousing space with no immediate plan regarding how much space would be needed, what it would be used for, or (most importantly) if the current leased space could be better utilized to not require the need for new space

With better space utilization and space management, all of the company's products could fit into one of the two facilities it leased. This would make possible increased efficiency of all operational staff by having all operations occur under one roof. The Interim COO eagerly presented the plan to consolidate and transform operations over a ninety-day period, followed by a ninety-day follow-on project to extend operational excellence to field installations and supporting administrative departments. All of these actions would result in an estimated $400,000-plus in annual savings, dropping right to the bottom line with less than $50,000 in expense.

The Interim was shocked when he was told by the CEO that he was not interested in executing such a broad change to the business. The company was hyper-profitable, and the changes outlined were perceived to be potentially painful. The company had struggled through some painful growth over the previous two years and did not have the appetite to take on such an aggressive initiative. As a result, it had very little impetus for change and was a poor fit in relation to the recommendations and approaches of the Interim.

The Interim helped the company remedy the issues in the middle of its processes as requested, but this fixed a relatively small problem and created very little bottom-line impact. This is a real-life example of a scenario where an Interim was not a good fit due to the company having no impetus to change.

BABYSITTERS AND PLACEHOLDERS

With the Interim revolution well underway in America, it is interesting that Interims frequently are not thought of as powerful leaders who embrace change and confidently lead organizations to higher results, but rather as titular placeholders. This is most often seen in press releases from publicly traded companies when some shock or unforeseen event has led to a sudden executive vacancy. Rarely are these announcements focused on the opportunities for change and transformation the Interim will address. Rather, these actions paint the Interim as a placated lapdog, guarding the seat until its rightful owner is named. If this is an organization's view of Interim leadership, then it is missing most of the value an Interim can bring to the assignment.

SITUATIONS WHERE LONG-TERM OWNERSHIP IS REQUIRED

Occasionally, situations arise where a company must have a permanent leader to ensure that clarity and stability exist during critical times. For example, a company in the midst of a life-threatening lawsuit or under investigation by a regulatory agency may be best served by waiting until a permanent leader is in place to ensure continuity in approach, strategy, and execution in such a critical situation.

This situation can also arise in executive roles that are highly specialized and core to the company's value chain or operational prowess. These roles could best be described as subspecialties of subspecialties. Interims often do not make sense in these situations because the population of candidates who could serve as excellent Interims may be tiny or even nonexistent. Organizations finding themselves in this situation may want to consider developing a transition plan by assigning those responsibilities internally or finding a consultant with skills in that discipline. An Interim or other internal executive can take over the leadership role until a full-time person is found.

SUMMARY

Interims exist to help companies surmount major challenges where the stakes and outcome truly matter. As significant change agents with a commitment to adding maximum value throughout an engagement, Interims show up ready to get to work with an expectation of proper authority and urgency to get results. Any company seriously considering searching for an Interim should be honest with itself to ensure that other types of assistance are not better suited for the company or its needs.

CHAPTER 12

LOCATE

FINDING AND ENGAGING AN INTERIM

Once an organization has determined that using the talents of an Interim is a solid notion, the questions quickly become ones of where to find and how to engage a qualified candidate. This chapter outlines the basics of locating, negotiating with, and contracting an Interim.

WHERE DO I FIND AN INTERIM?

The search for a qualified Interim Executive is not easily accomplished with traditional online search engines. In the Internet 1.0 era, companies gained more power taking employee recruitment online, attracting audiences using online job posting websites like Monster.com or Career Builder, which swelled with tens of millions of résumés.

The proliferation of online résumé submission caused corporate Human Resource (HR) departments to counter with automated filtering software designed to scan credentials by keyword. This new kind of arms war resulted in candidates spraying websites with résumés while skipping cover letters or personalization. Companies meanwhile processed vast amounts of information using algorithms and automation with minimal human touch or reply.

The rise of LinkedIn and its dominance as a tool to connect professionals resulted in it quickly becoming the default online résumé for professionals, especially executives, planet wide. LinkedIn, in its quest to monetize hundreds of millions of sets of credentials, morphed into a tool used by recruiters internally within corporate HR departments, and externally by independent executive search firms. Headhunters dedicated much of their time sifting through LinkedIn for permanent employment candidates, or for professionals that could be poached from their current job for the next best opportunity.

Legacy search tools created to facilitate permanent placement have several major challenges in providing meaningful results for companies searching online for interim, project, and fractional help. Part of the challenge is separating individuals who have simply restated their traditional executive experience as being Interim in nature, not understanding the differences and requirements of an Interim. Another is that platforms like LinkedIn are not optimal for sharing Interim engagements and experience, leaving users with high-level ideas about an Interim's experience, but often too few details to know if that person could be of help.

Further complicating the search is that, in some cases, true Interims haven't actually labeled themselves as such. Especially in the US, where the Interim specialty is still maturing, these individuals have resorted to labels such as "consultant" for lack of a better word to describe what they do. The idea of Interim leadership as a career is so nascent in America that there are individuals performing Interim work, unaware that a community of similar executives exists.

Searching for executive-level consultants typically results in a deluge of results that include professionals who focus more on giving great advice than executing on plans, diving headfirst into tough problems, and being held accountable for those results, all hallmarks of a true Interim. Organizations should also be aware of executives who may have job histories with positions of "Interim (fill in the blank)" in babysitter or placeholder roles (e.g. signing off on financial statements), versus the true career Interim specializing in *X-Formation* and change.

To further muddy the waters, the traditional résumé/CV format does not lend itself well to Interims who may have taken on so many assignments that they could end up publishing a tome if they spelled out each one. As a result, often an Interim's corporate entity will be listed on these documents, lumping together years of interim experience that span many different industries and positions into a single company and role with few details about their client work.

	Google	LinkedIn Jobs	LinkedIn Recruiter
Interim	99,800,000	9,523	1,261,677
Turnaround	47,200,000	6,395	458,658
Interim CEO	7,800,000	6	106,814
Interim CFO	1,200,000	24	60,222
Interim Executive	9,510,000	582	351,432

Search date April 5, 2017

Exhibit: Searching LinkedIn or Google for keywords "Interim," "turnaround," "Interim CEO," "Interim CFO," and "Interim Executive" shows both the small relative awareness of Interim as a profession and the large amount of information that needs to be sifted through in utilizing traditional search tools to locate Interim help.

Companies searching through results on LinkedIn or other search engines, should be careful to ensure each candidate demonstrates a history of measurable success executing transformative assignments. Each of these assignments should be in executive decision-making roles lasting three months to two years, where the Interim directly led execution and delivered positive results. Interims often will have started their careers in larger corporations and have launched new lines of business and turned around divisions within the parent company. Others may have built a company from scratch as an entrepreneur or led large scale transformation efforts as a senior consultant in a Big-6 type model.

An alternative to searching blindly is an online job posting. However, many Interims do not spend much time on job boards, which are typically flooded with permanent positions. If timing is on your side, an online job ad could be a good solution, but companies in an urgent or sensitive situation (i.e. turnaround) may need to be more proactive, not having the time to wait for applicants to show up. Further, many sites that are oriented toward project-based opportunities or "gigs" tend to have few executive opportunities.

In Europe, where Interim Executives have been common for decades, sites exist that are dedicated to Interim assignment postings, but companies still need to tread carefully to make sure they are getting the best quality Interim for the project versus trying to find the lowest bidder. Especially in down markets, the number of Interims accessing these sites may suddenly skyrocket as job seekers flood the market, trying to find a fill-in assignment while they search for their next permanent position.

Just as traditional online search tools leave a lot to be desired in the realm of Interim search, traditional placement agencies similarly fall short. In Europe, a multitude of Interim placement providers, associations, and institutes exist as a resource to local companies as the market is far more mature. In North

America, however, interim leadership is still evolving. A few permanent placement agencies have explored this new territory but have struggled to quickly identify and deploy Interim talent. Traditional placement firms expect a search to require six to nine months, require many interviews, personality profiling, and other lengthy activities in a process typically prone to long wait times between steps. Traditional recruiters are frequently used for the permanent search while the Interim is on board, but they rarely locate and place Interims in roles.

The challenges with these online and more mainstream resources demonstrate some of the reasons why the vast majority of Interims operate in a lone wolf fashion as diamonds-in-the-rough, finding most of their assignments through word-of-mouth or other high-impact, low-touch methods.

Some Interims choose to join small boutique firms with partners focusing on a particular business or industry. Larger specialized firms, such as those in the turnaround space, target the Fortune 500 with much higher price points. The vast majority of Interims, however, still function as solo operators. Therefore, InterimExecs, with its high quality and fully vetted membership base, serves as an excellent resource for companies that are starting a search. InterimExecs also provides placement for Interims, serving as another option for companies looking for help finding the right interim talent.

HOW TO NEGOTIATE AN AGREEMENT WITH AN INTERIM

The most productive negotiations are up-front and frank. The owner, board, investors, or CEO make an open and honest presentation concerning the issues or opportunities and what goals and expectations they have for the company and the Interim, as well as the budget for these activities. The Interim, in turn, responds with his or her normal rates, terms, and other details of a typical client engagement.

The first step in the negotiation process is establishing the company's desired start date and target time commitment, and the candidate's availability. Some Interims work on a dedicated full-time basis with one client at a time, while others work on a fractional basis, taking on multiple clients with varying time commitments in parallel. Either way, availability should be confirmed before other points are discussed.

Intense major *X-Formations* tend to be full time in nature. In many instances, turnaround work is full on and exclusive, not allowing any other concurrent work as the task at hand will require the full attention of the Interim. Therefore, if the Interim being considered could only add a fractional engagement at the current time, that person would not be good a fit, unless starting fractionally was a transition plan while the Interim transitioned out of other roles over an agreed upon period of time.

On the other hand, there are many scenarios where fractional or part-time assignments work for many reasons. In many startups, the team may not be fully formed, funding may not yet have been secured, or the company may simply only need an Interim's part-time help. Companies that are scaling up and expanding their executive team may not be able to assimilate the efforts of a full-time Interim. This often arises as companies grow and discover the need for, say, a technology executive (CIO/CTO), where two or three days per week are sufficient to move initiatives forward, work on new strategy and build plans. In these cases, the Interim could have multiple parallel engagements running simultaneously, and in many cases, Interims mix interim assignments with longer-term service on boards.

When it comes to establishing the terms and creating an agreement, veteran Interims have standard contracts that can be easily adapted to a particular company and its circumstances. The most common component will be cash-based fees for services. The rate is typically expressed as an hourly or daily fee, with weekly, monthly, or fixed fee arrangements also occurring, although fixed fee tends to only exist on very short engagements, or up-front analysis (or similar) projects that may be sold as a product. This approach is used in scenarios like performing a technology needs assessment where this information is necessary to understand the long-term assignment and what will be included before making a larger commitment. In many cases, the Interim will ask for a portion of his fee to be paid up front or as a retainer against future billing. Payment terms should also be clear, with due-upon-receipt terms tending to be the most common as Interims expect to stay current with their clients due to the important work they are performing.

If the engagement is long or involves significant potential for upside to the company, such as a dramatic cost savings, enhanced performance of key assets, or enabling a strategic revenue channel, an additional performance based fee is common. In cases where the Interim believes his or her efforts will result in a dramatic increase in enterprise value, equity, warrant, or other noncash compensation is often provided. Essentially, the bigger the stakes, the more extensive the compensation should be, provided the expected results are successfully delivered.

Usually the contract will have a short cancellation period, say thirty days, reflecting the nature of interim work. The agreement is not like a permanent employment contract and should not include severance (beyond the length of term or termination notice period) or any form of residual benefits. The agreement should make it relatively easy for all parties to exit—this is the nature of interim executive work.

> Because Interims believe in the go-anywhere-anytime mantra, work can commence within days—far faster than any standard permanent hiring process.

REFERENCES

Every candidate for an Interim assignment should be able to clearly articulate how he or she plans to address the needs set forth by the company, readily referencing specific scenarios where they addressed similar challenges, the tools and techniques used, lessons learned, and results delivered. Great caution should be exercised when assessing any applicant who is not able to supply adequate references or point to recent client accomplishments. To use a medical metaphor, if you need surgery, you don't go to the doctor who's operating for the first time, nor one who has not performed an operation in a long time.

Veteran Interims will supply references only as a final step in the process, since most references supplied will be busy company owners, board members, and executives who actively protect their time. Therefore, it is prudent for a company engaging an Interim to wait until the hiring of that Interim is essentially a done deal before contacting these important people for endorsements.

One possible exception to references involves Interims who specialize in turnarounds. These individuals often end up in the unenviable position of saving companies or assets at the expense of one or more stakeholders (employees, investors, lenders, bondholders, customers, or creditors). While the initial hiring party may be happy with the turnaround executive's services, salvage work may leave other parties unwilling to provide references.

SEALING THE DEAL

In many cases, Interims engage with an initial, short-term assessment or discovery project, lasting from a couple days to several weeks. This approach limits the risk the company takes in contracting with the Interim, and also allows the Interim an opportunity to determine if the project represents the best use of his or her skills and abilities. This frank assessment of the company and its current state creates a common understanding of the largest opportunities for *X-Formation*, allowing the company to assess the viability of the business, division, or opportunity. Up-front assessments like these should ideally create a standalone deliverable that includes findings and go-forward recommendations. Once clear, the company and the Interim can decide together how to proceed and in what capacity the Interim will be involved in executing the plan. Should the engagement end here, the company has gained a valuable work product it can use in executing internally driven changes.

Whether work begins with an assessment or an open-ended agreement, it will commence when the contract is signed and any other up-front terms are fulfilled. Because Interims believe in the go-anywhere-anytime mantra, work can commence within days—far faster than any standard permanent hiring process.

It is important to note that true Interims have all experienced significant success in their careers, and thus usually have other choices and opportunities for how they will spend their time and engage their abilities. Both the initial interview with an Interim, as well as subsequent interactions including any assessment or discovery period, are opportunities for the Interim to make go or no-go decisions regarding the company. Therefore, once both sides see the value in proceeding, the engaging company should work to move quickly to finalize terms and execute an agreement.

Organizations deciding to move forward with an Interim should be ready to maximize the benefits of an Interim's involvement, as outlined in Chapter 9: "Prepare," setting the stage for a positive *X-Formation*.

SUMMARY

Once an organization has confirmed its desire to find and engage an Interim Executive, the search for the right person can prove to be somewhat frustrating using traditional search firms and techniques. Interims tend to work as lone wolves, having nontraditional résumés and working tightly within their network or other closed communities, as compared to performing mass-market searches for opportunities.

InterimExecs, other specialized search firms, and a company's network are all tools that can be used to streamline the process of finding, interviewing, and ultimately engaging an Interim who can be of service. Once engaged, Interims will sometimes begin by performing a standalone up-front assessment of the company. This first assignment provides an excellent opportunity for the company to learn how the Interim works, validate that the anticipated results of *X-Formation* can be realistically attained, and achieve a good overall Interim/Client fit.

GLOSSARY

Note: Many of the terms in this glossary were adapted from Wikipedia.

Accountability Chart—Depicts the reporting structure of an organization from a functional standpoint and defines the roles for which each function is accountable. Includes the name and title for each position. Often described as an org chart on steroids.

Active Listening—A tool utilized by Interim Executives whereby they ask open-ended questions, attentively listen to responses, and repeat their understanding of the responses to ensure clarity and gain alignment with individuals and teams.

Bottom-Up Approach—The management practice or leadership style in which decisions are driven from employees or departments up to the executive ranks. Also describes a general process of looking at problems from the highest level of detail and smallest factors first and summing those smaller parts into a larger whole.

C-Suite—Another term for executive team.

Chief Academic Officer (CAO)—Responsible for academic administration at universities and other higher-education institutions.[19]

Chief Accounting Officer (CAO)—Responsible for overseeing all accounting and bookkeeping functions, ensuring that ledger accounts, financial statements, and cost control systems are operating effectively.

Chief Administrative Officer (CAO)—Responsible for business administration, including daily operations and overall performance.

Chief Analytics Officer (CAO)—Responsible for data analysis and interpretation.

Chief Architect (CA)—Responsible for designing systems for high availability and scalability, specifically in technology companies. Often called Enterprise Architect (EA).

---

19 Wikipedia, s.v., "List of Chief Officer (CxO) Titles," last modified December 1, 2017, https://en.wikipedia.org/wiki/Corporate_title.

Chief Artificial Intelligence Officer (CAIO)—Responsible for AI research department. Additionally sets AI strategy and defines viable AI products and solutions to organization.

Chief Audit Executive (CAE)—Responsible for the internal audit. This executive is often also responsible for overall compliance activities and organizational controls.

Chief Brand Officer (CBO)—Responsible for a [organization's] brand image, experience, and promise, and propagating it throughout all aspects of the company, overseeing marketing, advertising, design, public relations and customer service departments.

Chief Business Officer (CBO)—Responsible for the administrative, financial, and operations management of the organization, often combining the roles of Chief Administrative Officer (CAO), Chief Financial Officer (CFO), and Chief Operating Officer (COO).

Chief Business Development Officer (CBDO)—Responsible for development of plans designed to support business growth. Similar to Chief Revenue Officer, but sometimes more focused on greenfield opportunities or new channels/markets.

Chief Commercial Officer (CCO)—Responsible for the commercial strategy and the development of an organization.

It typically involves activities relating to marketing, sales, product development, and customer service to drive business growth and market share.

Chief Communications Officer (CCO)—Responsible for communications to employees, shareholders, media, bloggers, influencers, the press, the community, and the public.

Chief Compliance Officer (CCO)—Responsible for overseeing and managing regulatory compliance.

Chief Content Officer (CCO)—Responsible for developing and commissioning content (media) for broadcasting channels and multimedia exploitation.

Chief Creative Officer (CCO)—In one sense of the term, responsible for the overall look and feel of marketing, media, and branding. In another sense, similar to Chief Design Officer.

Chief Customer Officer (CCO)—Responsible for customer satisfaction and relationship management.

Chief Data Officer (CDO)—Responsible for enterprise-wide governance and utilization of information and data as assets, via data processing, data analysis, data mining, information trading, and other means.

Chief Design Officer (CDO)—Responsible for overseeing

all design aspects of a company's products and services, including product design, graphic design, user experience design, industrial design, and package design, and possibly aspects of advertising, marketing, and engineering.

Chief Development Officer (CDO)—Responsible for activities developing the business. Usually through added products, added clients, markets, or segments. Defines, develops, and optimizes new lines of business and owns and optimizes the value chain. Oftentimes leads integration efforts after an acquisition.

Chief Digital Officer (CDO)—Responsible for adoption of digital technologies, digital consumer experiences, the process of digital transformation, and devising and executing social strategies.

Chief Diversity Officer (CDO)—Responsible for diversity and inclusion, including diversity training and equal employment opportunity.

Chief Engineering Officer (CEngO)—Similar to the more common Chief Technology Officer (CTO); responsible for technology/product R&D and manufacturing issues in a technology company; oversees the development of technology being commercialized.

Chief Executive Officer (CEO)—Responsible for the overall

vision and direction of an organization, having ultimate authority over the entire organization as the highest-ranking management officer and often also the chairman of the board. Usually called CEO in the United States, Chief Executive or Managing Director in the United Kingdom and some other countries. Sometimes referred to as the Visionary.

Chief Experience Officer (CXO)—Responsible for user experience, overseeing user experience design and user interface design.

Chief Financial Officer (CFO)—Responsible for all aspects of finances and accounting. Provides financial strategy and oversight to the organization.

Chief Gaming Officer (CGO)—Responsible for both the game development and the online/offline publishing functions of a company that makes video games.

Chief Human Resources Officer (CHRO)—Responsible for all aspects of human resource management and industrial relations.

Chief Information Officer (CIO)—Responsible for information technology (IT), particularly in IT companies or companies that rely heavily on an IT infrastructure.

Chief Information Security Officer (CISO)—Responsible for information security.

Chief Innovation Officer (CIO)—Responsible for fresh thinking and providing often provocative and perception-changing ideas to a company.

Chief Investment Officer (CIO)—Responsible for investment and for the asset liability management (ALM) of typical large financial institutions such as insurers, banks, and pension funds.

Chief Information Technology Officer (CITO)—Responsible for information technology. Often equivalent to Chief Information Officer (CIO) and Chief Technology Officer (CTO).

Chief Knowledge Officer (CKO)—Responsible for managing intellectual capital and knowledge management.

Chief Learning Officer (CLO)—Responsible for training and career development.

Chief Legal Officer (CLO)—Responsible for overseeing and identifying legal issues in all departments, as well as corporate governance and business policy. Often called General Counsel (GC) or Chief Counsel.

Chief Manufacturing Officer (CMO)—Responsible for all

facets of manufacturing strategy, processes, and equipment, ultimately owning the quality of items produced and efficiency of manufacturing operation.

Chief Marketing Officer (CMO)—Responsible for marketing; job may include sales management, product development, distribution channel management, marketing communications (including advertising and promotions), pricing, market research, and customer service.

Chief Medical Officer (CMO)—Responsible for scientific and medical excellence, especially in pharmaceutical companies, health systems, hospitals, and integrated provider networks. The title is used in many countries for the senior government official who advises on matters of public health importance.

Chief Networking Officer (CNO)—Responsible for social capital within the company and between the company and its partners.

Chief Operating Officer (COO)—Responsible for business operations, including operations management, operations research, and (when applicable) manufacturing operations; role is highly contingent and situational, changing from company to company and even from a CEO to its successor within the same company. Often called "director of operations" in the nonprofit sector.

Chief Privacy Officer (CPO)—Responsible for all the privacy of the data in an organization, including privacy policy enforcement.

Chief Process Officer (CPO)—Responsible for business processes and applied process theory, defining rules, policies, and guidelines to ensure that the main objectives follow the company strategy as well as establishing control mechanisms.

Chief Procurement Officer (CPO)—Responsible for procurement, sourcing goods and services and negotiating prices and contracts.

Chief Product Officer (CPO)—Responsible for all product-related matters. Usually includes product conception and development, production in general, innovation, user experience, and project and product management. Sometimes defends the value proposition of individual products by recognizing and resisting instances where cost reduction or standardization efforts would impede it in ways that operations management may not fully recognize, such as after mergers and acquisitions.

Chief Production Officer (CPO)—Oversees and directs an entire production operation for a manufacturing organization. These professionals ensure quality and profitability of products generated in the production process.[20] More commonly referred to as Chief Manufacturing Officer.

Chief Quality Officer (CQO)—Responsible for quality and quality assurance, setting up quality goals, and ensuring that those goals continue to be met over time. In regulated industries, this person typically is responsible for compliance.

Chief Research and Development Officer (CRDO)—Plans and directs all aspects of an organization's research and development policies, objectives, and initiatives. Maintains an organization's competitive position and profitability by formulating research and development programs, policies, and procedures. Investigates and identifies new technologies that align with the organization's development.[21]

Chief Research Officer (CRO)—Responsible for all aspects of research for an organization, typically in industries that require deep and specialized research, analysis, and forecasting, such as financial newsletter publication.

Chief Revenue Officer (CRO)—Responsible for creating scalable and sustainable revenue strategies designed to align sales mix to goals, insulate the organization from risk,

---

20 Lucy Friend, "Job Description for a Productive Executive," *Careertrend.com,* July 25, 2017, https://careertrend.com/facts-6807962-job-description-production-executive.html.

21 "Top Research and Development Executive." *Salary.com,* 2017, http://swz.salary.com/salarywizard/Top-Research-and-Development-Executive-Job-Description.aspx.

and maximize enterprise value.[22] This position is popular in SaaS business models.

Chief Risk Officer (CRO)—Responsible for risk management, ensuring that risk is avoided, controlled, accepted, or transferred and that opportunities are not missed. Sometimes called Chief Risk Management Officer (CRMO).

Chief Sales Officer (CSO)—Responsible for increasing sales by designing the right strategy for each channel. A CSO is focused on strategy. This role works best in complex business environments with multiple channels, verticals, and competitors.[23]

Chief Science Officer (CSO)—Responsible for science, usually applied science, including research and development and new technologies. Sometimes called Chief Scientist.

Chief Security Officer (CSO)—Accountable for the development and oversight of policies and programs intended for the mitigation and reduction of compliance, operational, strategic, financial and reputational security risk strategies relating to the protection of people, intellectual assets, and

22 Jim Herbold, "The Rise of the Chief Revenue Officer: Silicon Valley's New Secret Sauce," *VB,* April 26, 2015, https://venturebeat.com/2015/04/26/the-rise-of-the-cro-silicon-valleys-new-secret-sauce/

23 Matt Sharrars, "The Difference between a Chief Sales Officer and VP of Sales," *SBI,* September 20, 2017, https://salesbenchmarkindex.com/insights/part-2-the-difference-between-a-chief-sales-officer-and-vp-of-sales/.

tangible property.[24] The definition of this position can vary greatly from one company to the next, particularly in regard to physical versus data/information security.

Chief Strategy Officer (CSO)—Responsible for strategy, usually business strategy, including strategic planning and strategic management. Assists the Chief Executive Officer with developing, communicating, executing, and sustaining strategy. Sometimes called Chief Strategic Planning Officer (CSPO).

Chief Sustainability Officer (CSO)—Responsible for environmental and sustainability programs.

Chief Technology Officer (CTO)—Responsible for technology research and development, overseeing the development of technology to be commercialized. (For an information technology company, the subject matter would be similar to the CIO's; however, the CTO's focus is technology for the firm to sell versus technology used for facilitating the firm's own operations.) Sometimes called Chief Technical Officer.

Chief Value Officer (CVO)—Ensures that all programs, actions, new products, services, and investments create and capture customer value.

---

24 Wikipedia, "Chief Security Officer," last modified September 4, 2017, https://en.wikipedia.org/wiki/Chief_security_officer.

Chief Visionary Officer (CVO)—Responsible for defining corporate vision, business strategy, and working plans. Sometimes called simply the Visionary.

Chief Web Officer (CWO)—Responsible for the web presence of the company and usually for the entire online presence, including intranet and internet (web, mobile apps, other).

Consultant—A person who provides expert advice professionally.

CXO—Chief Anything Officer. While exceedingly rare that one individual could fill any executive seat in an organization, this moniker describes an individual capable of filling one of several different C-level positions in an organization as an Interim Executive. Also, slang for an Interim Executive.

Death Spiral—The pattern in business where diminishing results (sales, bottom-line profits, or similar) create a negative feedback loop. As results diminish, fewer resources exist to influence a change. The company must either break the death spiral, or it will cease to be solvent or relevant in its markets.

Demand Innovation—Refers to the process of reinventing business processes and practices related to selling products or services. Term refers to the notion that a company never sells anything, rather it creates demand through marketing, positioning, and branding, then serves that demand, culminating in a sale.

Domain Expertise—Knowledge exhibited by an individual in specific subject areas. "Deep Domain Expertise" refers to the notion of an individual being an expert in areas that are highly specific.

EBITDA—Earnings Before Interest, Taxes, Depreciation, and Amortization. This measure provides a clearer picture of company performance and is typically used for valuation purposes during sale/merger/acquisition.

Economies of Scale—The optimization principle which dictates that some processes become more efficient (reduce unit costs) with increased volume. This is particularly true of companies that have high fixed costs.

End Run—Common corporate lingo describing the behavior where an employee goes to the ultimate decision-maker rather than following the chain of command and established processes for gaining approval for a decision.

Evolutionary Cycle—Business cycle characterized by incremental improvement. Evolutionary cycles end when critical barriers are encountered that cannot be overcome.

Executive—An individual having the power to put plans,

actions, and laws into effect. Or a person with senior managerial responsibility in a business organization.

Executive Team—Top level leadership of an organization, typically comprised of individuals with "Chief" or "Vice President" in their title. Also referred to as the C-suite.

Fractional Interim—An Interim Executive who works in a non-full-time capacity with an organization. For example, a two-day-a-week CIO, etc. Interims who work in a fractional capacity typically work with more than one client at a time.

Full-time Interim—An Interim Executive who works in a full-time capacity with an organization but is not an employee. As compared to fractional Interim Executives, these individuals tend to work with a single client at a time, devoting their full energy to that one company.

Gig Economy—Refers to the rapidly progressing personal economy where individuals become self-employed and work as specialized contractors who pick up "gigs" or assignments to earn a living.

Hierarchical Organization—A means of organizing employees within a company such that each employee reports to a given supervisor. All resources have a reporting chain that extends eventually to the CEO, who reports to the board of directors.

Interim Executive (aka Interim or Interim Exec)—An executive leader for a nonpermanent duration. Interim Executives receive the title and responsibilities of a permanent employee in the same position, but are not permanent holders of these positions, working either full-time or fractionally for a stated duration.

InterimExecs—An association devoted to the industry of Interim Executive leadership. Formerly known as the Association of Interim Executives, this organization maintains high standards for all members and is generally considered the premier professional membership organization for Interim Executives in America.

InterimExecs RED Team—The Rapid Executive Deployment (RED) Team is a select group of InterimExecs members who represent the top of the organization's membership. These individuals are qualified to be deployed by InterimExecs to clients in need of urgent transformation and assessment.

Interim *X-Formation* Disciplines—strategize, optimize, maximize, organize.

IP—Abbreviation for Intellectual Property.

IPO—Abbreviation for Input/Process/Output, or Initial Public Offering.

Leadership Team—At many organizations another name for executive team

Lean Manufacturing/Techniques—Philosophy developed in the 1980s by Toyota designed to harmonize production flow and reduce waste, thus increasing the efficiency and value of what is produced.

Management Consultant—An individual who helps organizations through analysis of existing organizational problems and develops plans for improvement.

Matrixed Organization—A manner of aligning employees whereby there is no permanent, full-time reporting structure of one individual to another. Rather, employees perform jobs that range across different managers depending on the work being performed.

Maximize—To make as large or great as possible. In the Interim world, this refers to the execution discipline of aligning sales and marketing activities with products, services, and support services to create the largest cost-effective volume of revenue. One of the four key *X-Formation* disciplines.

Mind Trash—Self-limiting approaches caused by past unpleasant experiences, assumptions of negative outcomes, or other factors that are not actually at play.

Net Promoter Score—An index ranging from -100 to 100 that measures the willingness of customers to recommend a company's products or services to others. It is used as a proxy for gauging the customer's overall satisfaction with a company's product or service and the customer's loyalty to the brand.[25]

Optimize—This *X-Formation* execution discipline focuses on creating process efficiency, optimizing costs and implementing tools that will support future scale. The main objective is to produce more efficiency, thus driving a primarily bottom-line impact.

Organic Growth—Company expansion through internally initiated actions, namely that accomplished without acquiring or merging with other entities to acquire new customers, products, capabilities, or revenue streams.

Organization (Org) Chart—Depicts the reporting structure for a company, along with titles and names.

Organize—This *X-Formation* discipline focuses activities on aligning people, processes, systems and assets to produce company-wide results. This final *X-Formation* step increases and solidifies gains reached in strategizing, optimizing, and maximizing activities.

---

25 Medallia, Bain & Company, Inc., 2017, www.medallia.com/net-promoter-score/.

Pocket Veto—Refers to the disruptive practice of team members attending a decision-making meeting in which they disagree with the proposed action but do not say so. Instead they leave the meeting and work against the initiative by refusing to support it or directing their staff in a different direction.

President—Responsible for company top- and bottom-line performance and integration of major business functions across the entire organization. The President's main function is to translate the CEO's vision into a reality through planning and execution. Sometimes referred to as the Integrator.

Process Improvement—Refers to the activity of making incremental improvements to processes within an organization.

Process Innovation—Refers to the activity of dramatically changing and improving processes within an organization. This approach often yields entirely new ways of doing business or executing key processes.

Recency—The length of time since an event. This notion is most often discussed in the context of customer interactions and combined with frequency to establish the strength of a customer relationship. For example, "How often does a customer visit?" (frequency), and "How long since their last visit?" (recency).

Revolutionary Cycle—Business cycle characterized by dramatic and often sudden improvement. Revolutionary cycles end when critical barriers are overcome by utilizing new and powerful approaches to attain new heights as major barriers are overcome.

Scope—Defines the boundaries for a task, project, or Interim Executive engagement, typically with areas that are off limits clearly spelled out. Proper scope definition is important to maximizing the focus and effectiveness of resources who may otherwise expend energy on less fruitful endeavors.

Six Sigma—At many organizations, this simply means a measure of quality that strives for near perfection. Six Sigma as a practice is a disciplined, data-driven approach and methodology for eliminating defects (driving toward six standard deviations between the mean and the nearest specification limit) in any process—from manufacturing to transactional and from product to service.[26]

Strategize—This *X-Formation* discipline is oriented toward creating, validating, and adapting strategies. The goal of these activities is to ensure a solid base exists upon which to build optimization, maximization, and organization plans.

Strategy—A framework of actions designed to achieve, and practices designed to support, an organization's vision.

---

26 Isixsigma, 2017, https://www.isixsigma.com/new-to-six-sigma/getting-started/what-six-sigma/.

S.M.A.R.T. Goals—S.M.A.R.T. refers to the best practice of making goals Specific, Measurable, Attainable, Realistic, and Time-bound. Setting a goal in this manner help ensure it is clear and the results can be concretely measured.

SWOT Analysis—A common facilitated exercise designed to identify a company, or group's, Strengths, Weaknesses, Opportunities, and Threats.

Top-Down Approach—The management practice or leadership style where decisions are handed from executives down through the ranks. Also describes a general process of looking at problems from the lowest level of detail or largest factors first (i.e. 50,000-foot view). Solutions are developed by taking the view down a layer at a time and breaking items into constituent parts.

Use Case—A list of actions or event steps, typically defining the interactions between a role (known in Unified Modeling Language as an actor) and a system, to achieve a goal. The actor can be a human or other external system.[27]

Value Chain—All activities from presales to customer service that directly impact the customer and customer satisfaction.

Vision—Guiding strategy and principles of an organization,

27 Wikipedia, "Use Case," last modified December 27, 2017, https://en.wikipedia.org/wiki/Use_case.

often extending far into the future. Typically developed and protected by the CEO or visionary.

X-Formation—The art and science of accomplishing major transformation in an organization by applying the four key disciplines of strategizing, optimizing, maximizing, and organizing to achieve difficult goals, improve overall performance, and attain a new desired state. Interim Executives are experts in *X-Formation*, helping companies reach previously unattainable goals daily.

ABOUT THE AUTHORS

DAMON NETH

Damon Neth is an entrepreneur, senior executive, and C-Level consultant with expertise in developing transformational business, technology, and operation strategies. His passion is leading teams to implement large-scale change.

Since the 1990s, Damon has worked as an Interim Executive to transform nearly fifty companies, ranging from start-ups to Fortune 500s, through strategies focused on operational excellence. In 2014, he founded CXO Service Co., a premium provider of Interim Executive Leadership to organizations looking for transformational change and next-level results.

Damon has founded six companies over a twenty-year period, spanning the industries of high-end professional services, eCommerce, retail, distribution, manufacturing, software, and technology. He has successfully led four acquisitions and several exits. Damon also mentors individuals and teams to help them gain sharp focus and obtain measurable results. He speaks on topics related to leadership, organizational excellence, developing strategies, and EOS, the Entrepreneurial Operating System.

WILLIAM MINCE

Bill is an experienced public company executive who has successfully grown organizations through organic development of new product lines and acquisition of both public and private entities. He has been on the due diligence and integration team for over thirty acquisitions. He is a results-driven leader with significant operational and margin-improving successes. He is now focused exclusively on providing organizational coaching and Interim Executive management. He holds fourteen patents and previously published *Up from the Crowd: Lessons to Help Managers Become Effective Leaders*. He has both a BSBA and an MBA and is available to speak at trade and professional meetings.

JAMES B. TRELEAVEN

Jim Treleaven is the President and CEO of Via Strategy Group, LLC (VSG). VSG advises CEOs, boards of directors, and other C-level executives on growth and turnaround strategies, M&A transaction, and serves in interim C-level roles. He is also an adjunct faculty member at the University of Illinois, Chicago, Department of Information and Decision Sciences. He has had a successful career in industry as the CEO of both public and private technology companies ranging in size from $40 to $500 million.

He received his BS in Computer Engineering from Case Western Reserve University, his MBA from the University of Minnesota, and his PhD in Management from Case. He has taught at Case, the University of Illinois, and has lectured at several other leading universities. He has published extensively in both refereed and popular journals. He is a frequent speaker and has been featured on CNN and the Financial News Network. He currently serves on the board of the Illinois Technology Association (ITA), the Chicago Engineers Foundation, the advisory boards of three graduate business schools, and on the boards of several private companies.